Finance
Without
Fear

James E. Kristy
Susan Z. Diamond

amacom
American Management
Associations

To Edie and Allan

*This book is available at a special
discount when ordered in bulk quantities.
For information, contact Special Sales Department,
American Management Associations, Publications Group,
135 West 50th Street, New York, NY 10020.*

Library of Congress Cataloging in Publication Data

Kristy, James E.
   Finance without fear.

   Includes index.
   1. Business enterprises--Finance. 2. Corporations--
Finance. I. Diamond, Susan Z. II. Title.
HG4026.K74   1984   658.1'5   83-45215
ISBN 0-8144-5776-2

Printing number
10 9 8 7 6 5 4 3 2 1

Preface

Finance has been defined as the science of managing money and other assets. Why, then, do so many businesspeople fear finance? One reason, we think, is the complexity of the subject and its mysterious jargon; another is a feeling deep within many of us that we *must* understand it if we are to get anywhere at all in the modern world; and another is the intimidation that the no-nonsense demeanor of many financial managers can engender in their colleagues.

That fear will disappear as soon as you become acquainted with finance. For you are, in fact, no stranger to the territory you are about to explore in this book. You began to understand income and expense with your first allowance, return on investment with your first savings account, supply and demand with your first job search. The basic principles you'll recognize at once; it's only the techniques, their application, and the specialized language that you need to acquire. To help you understand that language, we've included a comprehensive glossary that contains important financial terms discussed in the text. Terms that appear in the glossary are italicized in the text.

As the title implies, *Finance Without Fear* is designed for readers with little or no financial training but some business experience. Our emphasis is on practical application—on the ''how'' more than the ''why.'' Our goal is to enable you to communicate effectively with your company's finance department and to do your work in harmony with the company's financial goals.

We've divided *Finance Without Fear* into four parts. Part One, ''Accounting Basics,'' explains fundamental accounting terminology and principles. In Part Two, ''Financial Analysis,'' we show you how to evaluate a business from a financial standpoint. Part Three, ''Financial Management,'' discusses budgeting, cash and receivables management, and stock. ''Financing the Business,'' Part Four, explains the different options a company has for raising funds to use in growth and expansion.

The idea for this book came from the many seminars for nonfinancial managers, administrative assistants, and secretaries that we both teach. The participants in those sessions provided invaluable guidance as to which needs and concerns *Finance Without Fear* should address. Our thanks also go to the AMACOM staff, in particular to Rob Kaplan, our editor, who truly showed the patience of Job on this project.

James E. Kristy
Susan Z. Diamond

Contents

PART ONE

Accounting Basics

Chapter 1

Introducing the Finance Department

Accounting has often been called "the language of business." But this metaphor goes too far if *language* is defined as a means of communicating thoughts and feelings as well as information. Accounting communicates only data or information, so it resembles a system of shorthand more than a language.

However, this does not detract from the importance of accounting. Most businesses involve a blizzard of transactions—buying, selling, making, spending, hiring, and so forth. One huge task of accounting is to record the financial aspects of these transactions. What's more, every transaction is a give-and-take with two sides to it—that is, an exchange of one thing for another. So the volume of data recorded is at least double the number of transactions.

To take just one simple example, every time you come to work, you create a financial transaction. The company gets the use of your time and talent and, in return, gives an unspoken promise to pay you for them on the next payday. And while you are at work, you are probably creating dozens more transactions, all of which have to be recorded—twice.

ACCOUNTING'S TWO PRINCIPAL TASKS

Accounting has two main jobs. It must record transactions and fit the variety of business activities into neat, manageable categories, *and* it must arrange these data into meaningful form for management to interpret. Managers seem to spend half their time asking questions: How much did we sell today? How much did we spend? How many employees do we have? And the most fundamental question: How profitable are we? Accounting provides the answers, and there is a real skill to doing it in a way that is easy to understand.

The word *control* is often used to describe the accounting function. We speak of "accounting control" and the company's "controller." But when we use *control* to refer to accounting's task of gathering and organizing information for management, it does not mean restricting or directing the firm's activities. Instead, it means obtaining and conveying the information managers need to make intelligent decisions about the activities. For example, the accounting department would not try to tell a salesperson how many miles to drive each day. But accounting might ask for a log of the miles driven by the person, total the auto expense for the month, list it in comparison with the figures for other salespeople, and perhaps calculate the ratio of sales dollars to miles driven by each person. That is the extent of accounting control.

The rest is up to management. Having read the accounting reports, management might question those salespeople with the highest mileage figures, praise those with the best sales-to-miles ratios, or redesign the reimbursement policy to give a smaller allowance. That is management control.

THE FINANCE DEPARTMENT

Now you may be saying to yourself, "In our company, there's a finance department, not an accounting department. What, if anything, is the difference?" The distinction between the two is somewhat nebulous, but usually finance encompasses accounting *plus* a number of other functions. These include managing the company's funds in the most efficient and profitable manner, determining the financial pros and cons of various investment options, and planning for the organization's future financial needs. Finance implies an active role in corporate decision making, while accounting is simply the recording and reporting of financial data.

WHO'S WHO IN FINANCE AND ACCOUNTING

The titles and duties of financial personnel vary somewhat from business to business, depending on the size of the firm, the abilities and the pecking order of the people involved, and the company's degree of financial sophistication. However, the following positions and their descriptions are fairly standard.

Most companies designate a *chief financial officer* (CFO) to manage all the accounting and financial specialists. In many companies, this individual has the rank of vice president. The CFO explains and interprets the financial reports to high-level executives and the board of directors. The CFO deals with the many outsiders concerned with the firm's finances, including shareholders, certified public accountants (CPAs), government agencies, bankers, and stockbrokers. The CFO also participates in major business decisions and is expected to know the financial impact of proposals dealing with every aspect of the business, including such diverse areas as marketing, production, and personnel.

The *treasurer* is concerned primarily with the company's money—what the company has now and what it will need in the coming weeks, months, and years. Cash flows in and out in a swiftly running stream—in from customers and out to employees, suppliers, and the government (as taxes). To run out of cash for even a short period can be not only a great inconvenience but a serious risk, so cash management requires constant attention. The treasurer may also be responsible for the firm's insurance needs, pension and stock plans, and credit function.

The *controller* (sometimes spelled "comptroller," but even then pronounced "controller") is the chief accounting officer. In many companies the controller is also a senior executive who participates in policy making. As keeper of the financial data, the controller is called on constantly for this or that report. However, with the increasing use of computers, specialists are emerging in "management information systems" (MIS). This function may be either under the controller or on the same level as the controller.

Another position that deserves special mention is the *internal auditor*—a sort of in-house accounting bloodhound who goes through company records and documents, trying to sniff out serious mistakes or wrongdoing. To prevent undue influence on the internal auditor from managers in the company, he or she may report directly to the president or even the board of directors. In some companies, the internal auditor also investigates nonfinancial areas to ensure that all company functions are performed in an efficient, economical, and ethical manner. This broadening of the internal auditor's responsibilities is due in large part to the Foreign Corrupt Practices Act of 1977 (FCPA), which requires companies to maintain strict controls over all financial practices. (For this reason, the FCPA is sometimes jokingly called the Internal Auditors' Full Employment Act.)

Internal auditors should not be confused with the firm's external auditors. The latter is an outside firm of CPAs that audits the company's financial statements before they are published in the annual report. We'll discuss the external auditor's role in later chapters.

Other important positions in the financial area include the director of financial planning, who is charged with preparing detailed financial plans and budgets; the tax manager, who copes with the myriad tax laws, always seeking the best legal way of minimizing tax expense; and the credit manager, who is responsible for approving customer credit and collecting the money owed by customers.

Another newly emerging specialist is the *financial analyst,* who makes lengthy and sophisticated studies of areas for company expansion, lease-versus-buy decisions, and other investment options. The *cost accountant* looks at the firm's operations—such as manufacturing or service—and analyzes the cost of labor, materials, and overhead for each type of product or activity.

It's obvious what the *payroll supervisor* does. There are also supervisors of *accounts receivable* (the money owed to the company), *accounts payable* (the money owed by the company), and the *general ledger* (the company's official book of accounts).

The value of these people can't be laid to the revenues they generate—for that is little or none. Someone must keep track of essential records, of course, but the real worth of the accounting and financial staff is in keeping management informed about the direction in which the company is heading and in estimating the financial consequences of proposed undertakings. Without this assistance, a company's president would be like the pilot of a ship trying to navigate in a thick fog without radar.

Chapter 2

The Double-Entry Accounting System

The double-entry accounting system is not a new idea; it originated in northern Italy some time before 1340. Catholic monks recorded and refined the principles and taught them to laymen. The Church also gave us many of the standard terms used today, such as *debit, credit,* and accounting *clerk* (the last comes from the word *cleric*). So ingenious was this system that it has remained in use virtually intact for over 600 years, in spite of the efforts of countless accountants and businesspeople to improve on it.

The basic principle of the double-entry system is that every transaction involves both give and take—as when a company spends $100 and receives $100 worth of goods or services. Double-entry accounting efficiently records this two-sided effect. Because both aspects are recorded simultaneously, we are able to find out a firm's financial condition whenever it suits us—even daily, if necessary.

Even in this age of automation, the recording of transactions always involves a piece of paper, such as a check request, sales slip, invoice, or time card. This basic document provides an ''audit trail,'' or reference back to the person who initiated the transaction. Many corporate procedures requiring forms and approvals have been designed to ensure personal accountability for all changes in the company's financial status.

Today computers store more and more of the data that used to be kept in file cabinets. One of the problems accompanying this development is maintaining the ability to trace every entry back to its origin. Without that ability, an organization is very vulnerable to covered-up mistakes and white-collar crime. To cope with this problem, companies set up elaborate internal audit procedures and systems of cross-checks.

THE FIVE BASIC CATEGORIES OF ACCOUNTS

With the double-entry system, both the give and the take aspects of the business's many transactions are neatly divided into five basic categories of accounts. These are assets, liabilities, equity, revenues, and expenses.

Assets and Liabilities

Assets are the financial, physical, and sometimes intangible properties used to make the business run. Cash, receivables, inventory, buildings, equipment, and land are all examples of assets. Each of these types of assets would have its own accounts in the company's books.

Liabilities are the debts and other obligations of a business—the money it has borrowed or the bills it has not yet paid.

In Chapter 3 we'll examine the various types of assets and liabilities in more detail.

Equity

Equity, sometimes called *net worth,* represents the amount of the owners' or shareholders' interest in the business. This is the permanent capital of the company.

In a corporation, the equity category comprises two types of accounts. The first type—Capital Contribution Accounts—shows the money received by the firm when it issued its shares of stock. These accounts will also be discussed in detail in Chapter 3. The second type of equity account—Retained Earnings—includes all the earnings or profits kept in the business since the company began. In other words, retained earnings are the portion of the company's profits that were reinvested instead of paid out to the shareholders in dividends. The figure in the Retained Earnings account represents the dollar value of all the assets that were acquired from these profits. The Retained Earnings account is not a cash fund; remember, Cash is an asset account.

The equity of unincorporated businesses—that is, sole proprietorships (single owners) or partnerships—has two accounts for each owner: "Capital" and "Draw." The Capital account records the amount each person invested in the business, including his or her share of retained profits. The Draw account, a negative figure, is the amount taken out of the business by the owner for his or her personal use. The Draw account is accumulated until the end of the year, when it is subtracted from Capital and set back to zero.

Revenues and Expenses

Revenues are the monies received or due from customers. Strictly speaking, they represent the value (in the form of goods or services) of what the company has *given* to its customers. But we usually think and speak of revenues in terms of what the firm *receives* in return from its customers—the amount of cash or accounts receivable. In most firms, revenues are called sales; but a bank will refer to its interest income, a consulting firm to its fees, and a real estate agency to its rents and commissions.

Expenses are the costs of running the business. The most significant expense account is usually Cost of Goods Sold—that is, the cost of the labor, materials, and overhead needed to make the product or to perform the service. Other typical accounts are General and Administrative (G&A) Expenses, Marketing Expenses, Interest, and Income Tax.

ASSETS AND EXPENSES

It may seem odd, but assets and expenses are rather similar. Nearly every expenditure the firm makes results in either an asset or an expense. (The only type of expenditure that does not translate into either an asset or an expense is the repayment of debt, which results, instead, in the reduction of a liability.) What determines the expenditure's account category is whether the item purchased will be consumed in the current year or will last longer. Goods or services that are used up immediately, such as employee labor, office supplies, and rent, are classified as expenses. Goods that last beyond the current year, such as trucks, word-processing equipment, and machinery, are listed as assets. Their cost is "written off," or expensed, proportionately each year through *depreciation*—a process we'll discuss further in Chapter 7.

Whether an expenditure results in an asset or an expense can be important to management. Expenses have an immediate impact in that they reduce a company's current profits and, possibly shareholders' dividends, management bonuses, and so on. At the same time, the greater the expenses, the less the company must pay in taxes—and companies, like individuals, try to keep Uncle Sam's share to a minimum. The cost of assets, in contrast, is spread over their useful life, and so has less dramatic effects on profits and taxes.

DEBITS AND CREDITS

The accounting profession's use of the terms *debit* and *credit* is about as helpful to humankind as the typical legal document filled with Latin phrases and obscure terminology. Such "professional language" confuses the issues, making people more dependent on the "experts," and does little else—unless you count the opportunities for writers and teachers to explain it all.

The terms derive from the Latin *debitum* ("debt") and *creditum* ("something entrusted"). These meanings only add to the confusion, as they reinforce our traditional idea that debits are something we owe and credits are something that is owed or due us. Unfortunately, in accounting, these meanings are not always appropriate. For example, when the company owes money, the appropriate liability account has a *credit* balance, and when the debt is paid, the account is *debited*. Consequently, the best approach is to pretend you've never heard the words *debit* and *credit* before and simply learn their accounting meanings the same way you'd learn the meanings of any other new terms.

The company's accounts all have dollar values, called *balances*. For example, the company's Inventory account may have a balance of $350,000, indicating that that sum is the dollar value of the inventory at that time. This and the sums in other accounts also have another characteristic, unstated and unknown except to the initiated (a group you are about to join!): They are either debit balances or credit balances. Asset and expense accounts have debit balances, while liability, equity, and revenue accounts all have credit balances. The debit balance accounts represent that which is owned (assets) or has been received (expenses) by the company. Credit balance accounts are monies owed (liabilities and equity) or goods given to others (sales and other revenues).

These balances are changed by the accounting entries that record each day's transactions. Every account, regardless of whether it has a debit or a credit balance, can be subject to either a debit or a credit entry, depending on the nature of the transaction. When a debit entry is made to a debit balance (or a credit entry to a credit balance), the balance increases. When a credit entry is made to a debit balance (or a debit entry to a credit balance), the balance decreases by the amount of the new entry.

Before we illustrate these principles, you need to become acquainted with the accountant's favorite means of illustration—the **T account.** The T account is not an official accounting form, but a device frequently used to teach accounting and to help accountants analyze or explain entries. The T account simply illustrates the debit and credit transactions of an account. A cardinal rule of accounting is that debits are always placed on the left-hand side of the T and credits are always placed on the right-hand side. So, in the following example, Cash account has a debit balance of $100,000.

Cash

100,000 |

This debit balance is normal because Cash is an asset account. When cash is paid out in a transaction, such as the purchase of a $10,000 piece of equipment, the entry to record that fact will contain a credit to Cash. That credit entry reduces the Cash account balance to $90,000:

Cash

100,000 | 10,000

If cash comes into the business, then a debit entry is made and the balance increases. In this case an additional $20,000 increases the Cash account balance to $110,000:

Cash

100,000 | 10,000
20,000 |

We mentioned at the beginning of this chapter that the double-entry system records both the give and the take of every transaction. Consequently, each entry made to record a transaction has equal amounts of debits and credits. With the purchase of a $10,000 piece of equipment, not only would we credit the Cash account with $10,000, but we would also debit the other account involved with the $10,000—in this case, Equipment:

DEBIT +	CREDIT −	DEBIT +	CREDIT −
Cash		**Equipment**	
100,000	10,000	10,000	

Likewise, the total of all debit balances must always equal the total of all credit balances. This principle—that debits and credits must always be equal—is essential to the system, and those furrows on your accountant's brow were probably etched by the effort made to keep the two values in balance.

Before we leave the world of debits and credits, let's review the basic principles. Asset and expense accounts have debit balances. Consequently, increases in assets and expenses are debits and decreases are credits. Liability, equity, and revenue accounts have credit balances. Therefore, increases in these accounts are credits and decreases are debits.

One last debit/credit item: Accountants frequently use the abbreviations for these terms. *Credit* is logically abbreviated *Cr.,* and *debit* is rather illogically abbreviated *Dr.*

ENTRIES TO THE JOURNAL

Accountants employ two "books" for recording business activity. Nowadays these "books" are likely to be computer files, but we still call them by their old names. The first is the *journal,* a financial diary in which every transaction of the business is recorded in chronological order. Figure 2-1 gives some simple examples showing how journal entries are made. Notice that in each case the debits equal the credits and both the give and the take of each transaction are recorded.

Even with the succinct form used by accountants, recording every transaction quickly becomes a burden. One way to ease the pain is to establish special journals for those types of entries that occur frequently. Thus most companies have a *cash receipts journal* to record transactions

Figure 2-1.   Sample entries in journal.

```
(a)  A company is formed with the issuance of $100,000 in stock:
        (Dr.) Cash                          100,000
        (Cr.)     Common stock                          100,000
(b)  Salaries totaling $1,100 are paid:
        (Dr.) Salary expense                  1,100
        (Cr.)     Cash                                    1,100
(c)  A typewriter is purchased for $1,400, $250 down with the balance
     due in 90 days:
        (Dr.) Office equipment                1,400
        (Cr.)     Cash                                      250
        (Cr.)     Accounts payable                        1,150
(d)  The first week's sales are recorded:
        (Dr.) Cash                            1,230
        (Dr.) Accounts receivable            14,660
        (Cr.)     Sales                                  15,890
```

involving incoming cash. Similarly, a company is likely to have a *cash payments journal,* a *purchases journal,* and a *sales journal.*

Recording activities as they occur works very well for gathering data, but problems arise when you want to retrieve the information. Retrieving data from a journal is like looking through last year's diary to find out how many times you had lunch with someone. You have to scan the entire book to get the answer. So to make the information more readily available, accountants transfer, or *post,* the journal data to the second book of account, the ledger.

POSTING TO THE LEDGER

In the *ledger,* each account has its own page. When records of transactions are posted from the journal to the ledger, all entries relating to the same account wind up on the same page. Therefore, all the entries—both debits and credits—to the asset account Office Equipment are grouped together for handy reference. A separate page or section is provided for each account in the five categories—assets, liabilities, equity, revenues, and expenses.

Obviously, a large company may have thousands of accounts. For example, each department may have an Office Supplies account as one

Figure 2-2.   Sample T accounts.

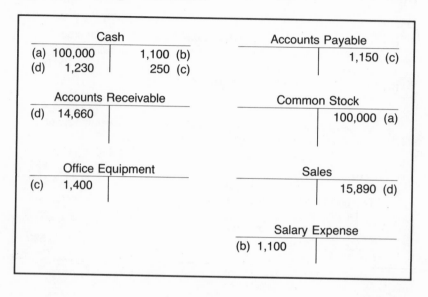

of its expense accounts. This type of detailed information breakdown makes it easy to review not only the department's office supplies expense but also the company's total expense in this area and the department's total expenses in all areas, And, of course, electronic data processing greatly simplifies all the computations.

Our friend the T account is sometimes used to represent a ledger page. The T accounts in Figure 2-2 show how the journal entries made in Figure 2-1 would be posted to the ledger.

Within the same T account or ledger page, each posting creates a new balance, either debit or credit, in the account. In the Cash T, for example, the debits total $101,230 and the credits come to $1,350; the account therefore has a debit balance of $99,880.

THE TRIAL BALANCE

Whenever a company wants financial statements (usually monthly), the balances are figured for all the accounts and listed on a report called the *trial balance*. The dollar amounts of each account are placed in the appropriate debit or credit column, as shown in Figure 2-3.

The term *trial balance* refers to the comparison of first-run totals of

Figure 2-3.   Sample trial balance.

TRIAL BALANCE
As of Year-End 1984

		Debits	Credits
Assets	Cash	$ 38,933	
	Accounts Receivable	120,371	
	Inventory	133,237	
	Prepaid Expenses	17,200	
	Investments	8,020	
	Property, Plant, and Equipment	365,737	
	Accumulated Depreciation		$ 186,985
	Goodwill	14,507	
	Other Assets	2,010	
Liabilities	Notes and Loans Payable		2,481
	Accounts Payable		59,145
	Accrued Liabilities		57,889
	Income Taxes Payable		27,319
	Long-Term Debt		49,160
	Deferred Taxes		20,778
Equity	Preferred Stock		13,006
	Common Stock		8,659
	Additional Paid-In Capital		98,014
	Retained Earnings		133,413
Revenues	Revenue		718,104
	Other Income		6,977
Expenses	Cost of Sales	557,001	
	Selling, G&A Expense	64,695	
	Interest Expense	5,056	
	Income Tax	47,200	
	Dividends	7,963	
		$1,381,930	$1,381,930

debit and credit columns. Since all the entries that comprise the individual account balances had (or should have had) equal amounts of debits and credits, the two columns of the trial balance should balance too. However, there are those who come up with unequal totals for the debit and credit columns. They say *trial* balance refers to the trials and tribulations of getting the %&*¢& thing to balance!

In all events, balance it must, for it is from this intermediate statement that the principal financial statements are prepared. Notice that the accounts in Figure 2-3 are listed by category—assets first, then liabilities, equity, revenues, and expenses. As you'll see in Chapter 3, the first three categories will be used in preparing the balance sheet, the last two in the income statement.

A trial balance is something you seldom see unless you work in an accounting department. But the financial statements prepared from it are essential tools of management. And because they offer a financial portrait of the firm, they are also of interest to the business's customers, suppliers, creditors, and investors.

Chapter 3

Financial Reports

Financial reports come in a variety of sizes, shapes, and styles, and the ultimate effect of this disparity is both a blessing and a curse. The blessing is the imaginative design and even artistic splendor of some annual reports such as Kodak's, Marshall Field's, and McCormick's (complete with spice scent). The curse is that the imaginative approach sometimes affects the financial statements—not the actual values, but the titles and placement of accounts and the way items are condensed. As a result, the hardest part of reading and interpreting a financial report—once you have learned what to look for—is *finding* the data you want in the report.

Some items are standardized. An annual report always contains a balance sheet and an income statement (sometimes masquerading under another name), and usually includes a statement of changes in financial position. In addition to these three statements, the report may include several charts, schedules, and footnotes that purport to explain the statements more fully but in fact may confuse the reader or alter the report's emphasis.

For most purposes, you can judge a company's success and strength by its balance sheet, income statement, and statement of changes *if* you know what to look for. In this chapter we'll describe these key statements, and in Chapter 8 we'll discuss their interpretation.

THE BALANCE SHEET

The *balance sheet* states the company's financial position on a particular day—usually the last day of a month or year. It has three main sections: assets, liabilities, and equity. As you'll recall from Chapter 2, assets are the money and physical properties that the company *owns,* while liabilities are the debts the company *owes. Equity* is the difference between the assets and the liabilities, or the net worth of the company, all of which belongs to the owners or shareholders. Therefore, the relationship among the three elements is:

$$Assets = liabilities + equity$$

or

$$Assets - liabilities = equity$$

The balance sheet acquired its name because the dollar amounts for these three items always balance out exactly according to this equation—which is so basic that it is known as *the accounting equation.*

Another equality is the balance of debits and credits. The values for assets are debits; those for both liabilities and equity are credits. Here the credits represent the sources of money coming into the business, and the debits show how the money is being used.

Assets

Running a business requires people, money, and things—or, to be more formal, human resources, financial resources, and physical properties. No way has been found to show the value of a company's managers and employees in its financial statement, but its physical properties and financial resources are included in the statement as the assets.

Assets are listed on the balance sheet according to their *liquidity*—that is, the time ordinarily required to convert them to cash. Those assets expected to convert to cash within a year are called current assets and are listed first. Cash, the most liquid of assets, heads the list of current assets. The slower-to-convert assets, or noncurrent assets, are next, including real estate, plant, and equipment, which are expected to convert to cash in more than a year or not to convert at all.

Let's look at the assets shown on the General Instrument Corporation's 1979 and 1980 balance sheets (Figure 3-1). For its own conve-

Figure 3-1. Balance sheet for General Instrument Corporation.

Consolidated Balance Sheet   General Instrument Corporation and Subsidiaries

February 29, 1980 and February 28, 1979

	1980	1979
Assets		
Current assets:		
Cash and temporary investments	$ 38,932,974	$ 64,524,100
Accounts receivable, less allowance for doubtful accounts of $4,600,000 and $4,300,000	120,371,418	98,928,084
Inventories:		
Materials and work-in-process	92,164,323	67,992,696
Finished goods	41,072,918	30,707,583
	133,237,241	98,700,279
Deferred income taxes	11,034,000	5,949,000
Prepaid expenses	6,165,969	3,691,417
Total current assets	309,741,602	271,792,880
Investments, advances and receivables due after one year	8,020,391	14,981,571
Property, plant and equipment, at cost	365,736,423	291,988,224
Less accumulated depreciation	186,984,903	171,181,079
	178,751,520	120,807,145
Cost in excess of net assets of purchased businesses	14,506,789	15,005,248
Other assets	2,009,854	2,275,493
	$513,030,156	$424,862,337
Liabilities and Stockholders' Equity		
Current liabilities:		
Notes and loans payable	$ 120,870	$ 4,254,807
Accounts payable	59,144,502	39,438,396
Accrued liabilities	57,888,822	45,084,958
Income taxes	27,319,423	23,050,069
Long-term debt due within one year	2,359,644	309,949
Total current liabilities	146,833,261	112,138,179
Long-term debt	49,160,293	71,844,534
Deferred taxes and other non-current liabilities	20,778,181	10,241,192
Stockholders' equity:		
Cumulative convertible preferred stock without par value, shares authorized: 2,000,000; shares outstanding: 520,243 and 520,258	13,006,075	13,006,450
Common stock, $1.00 par value, shares authorized: 15,000,000; shares outstanding: 8,658,665 and 7,820,859	8,658,665	7,820,859
Additional paid-in capital	98,013,586	76,398,244
Retained earnings	176,580,095	133,412,879
Total stockholders' equity	296,258,421	230,638,432
	$513,030,156	$424,862,337

See accompanying notes.

nience, a company can end its financial year (called a *fiscal year*) on any day of the calendar year; General Instrument's year-end is the last day of February.

Cash and Temporary Investments

Companies often have extra cash that won't be needed for a few days or weeks. They put these funds into *short-term, or temporary, investments* (sometimes called marketable securities) such as savings accounts, certificates of deposit, government securities—any investment that is safe, liquid, and interest-paying. Since $20 million invested at 12 percent interest (annual rate) will earn $6,575 per day, investing excess cash, even for a very short period, is worth the effort.

Accounts Receivable, Less Allowance for Doubtful Accounts

When a customer buys something but doesn't pay immediately, the amount of the purchase is added to the company's *accounts receivable*. Some of the receivables will never be collected, so an estimated amount is deducted as an "allowance for doubtful accounts" when the sale is made. Later, when the bad debts become known, the allowance is adjusted to match the actual loss. After cash and temporary investments, accounts receivable are the company's most liquid asset; hence they are usually second in the list of assets.

Inventories

If the company is a manufacturer, its inventories are divided into three types.

1. *Raw materials.* Raw materials are not just basic materials in crude form, such as iron ore, but *any* materials or parts purchased from others and made or put into the company's products.
2. *Work-in-process.* This refers to products that have been started but that are not yet finished. Note that General Instrument has combined the first two inventory categories as "materials and work-in-process."
3. *Finished goods.* These are products that are completed and ready for sale. If a company (such as a wholesaler or a retailer) does not do any manufacturing, all of its inventory will be finished goods. And, of course, a service company will have little or no inventory.

Deferred Income Taxes

The profit shown on a firm's financial statement often differs from that shown on its tax return because of special deductions the government allows and tax additions it imposes. Most of the differences are matters of timing. A company either avoids a tax payment now (by using accelerated depreciation, for example) and makes it up in later years or vice versa.

When *deferred income taxes* are shown as an asset, it means that the taxes have been paid but will not show up as an expense on the income statement until later because of the difference in tax and financial statement calculations. Note that there is also a liability account called Deferred Taxes. Here the taxes have been deducted on the income statement but won't actually be paid until some future year. Since the company still owes this money, it is a liability.

Prepaid Expenses

The *prepaid expenses* heading includes any rent, interest, insurance, taxes, and so on paid in advance. Although these assets will not be turned into cash, they are shown as current assets because they would have been cash if the company had not paid them in advance.

Noncurrent Assets

Noncurrent assets are grouped in these major categories: fixed, intangible, and all others.

Fixed Assets. "Property, plant, and equipment" are also called *fixed assets.* They are put on the books at their original cost and stay at that value until disposed of. With the exception of land, these assets depreciate in value through use, the passage of time, or some other circumstance. When such an asset is acquired, the company estimates the future depreciation. Each year, the company depreciates the item by an appropriate portion of the total depreciation. This annual depreciation is accumulated from year to year and is deducted from the original cost to obtain a *book value,* or *net property value.*

Recently, this method of valuing fixed assets has been criticized because it doesn't take into account the increase in property values due to inflation or the much higher replacement costs of plants and equipment. Suppose, for example, a firm built a small office building in 1950 for $40,000 and expected it to last 40 years. If $1,000 of depreciation was accumulated each year, by 1980 the building would have a book value of $10,000. On the market, however, the building might be worth many times the book value if it had been well maintained and was in a desirable location.

Accountants are still trying to find an acceptable way of showing current values. Some companies now issue two financial statements—an official one with historical costs and another one with the estimated current values of the assets. The latter statement may seem more realistic; however, a good case can be made for using historical costs by arguing the following points:

- The historical cost is the *actual* money the company had to pay for the property or equipment; current values often give the impression that the company invested much more. Current values are only estimates, and estimates vary even among expert appraisers. Also, appraised values and actual sale prices often differ greatly, as the owners of real estate and fine jewelry can testify.
- Since most companies intend to use up their plant and equipment, the balance sheet value is mainly intended to show how much of the cost has yet to be depreciated.
- Because companies are constantly buying new equipment, the historical costs actually contain some current values.
- Perhaps most important, the value of a firm's assets is ultimately reflected in the profit it makes, not in someone's guess as to what its building could be sold for.

Intangible Assets. "Cost in excess of net assets of purchased businesses" is considered an *intangible asset*. This mouthful of a title is often referred to informally as *goodwill*. It occurs when one company buys the assets of another company and pays more for them than their stated value or fair market value. For example, if Company A's assets had a balance sheet value of $1 million, and Company B bought them for $1.2 million, the extra $200,000 would be listed as "cost in excess . . ." or "goodwill."

Other intangible assets include nonphysical assets that represent rights to future benefits, such as patents, licenses, and trademarks. A third kind of intangible asset, the deferred charge (or expense), is any expense that is expected to have some future value to the company. Examples include payments for a magazine advertisement that has yet to be published and the expense of moving a business to larger quarters.

All Others. "Investments, advances, and receivables due after one year" and "other assets" belong in one "all others" category. Investments may be the common stocks of other companies the firm either is affiliated with or has an interest in. Advances are loans to subsidiary or affiliated companies or, possibly, to customers that are not expected to convert to cash within a year. Receivables due after one year are exactly what the name implies. "Other assets" is a catchall category for minor items that do not qualify for the other asset headings.

Liabilities

Where does the company get the money to buy assets? From the accounting equation (assets = liabilities + equity), you can see that part of the money comes from the firm's various creditors (the liabilities on the balance sheet). Like assets, liabilities are either current or noncurrent. Current liabilities are debts that fall due within one year of the financial statement date. Liabilities payable after a year are listed in the noncurrent section until one year of their due date, at which time they become current liabilities.

Notes and Loans Payable

Here *notes* means promissory notes, the "For value received, I promise to pay . . ." type of document. Usually notes are loans from banks, finance companies, insurance companies, or affiliated firms. Although they are debts due within 12 months, they are often part of a revolving, or renewing, credit arrangement whereby the loan, instead of being paid, is renewed for either the same or a different amount.

Accounts Payable

Most of the materials, supplies, and services a company purchases are bought on credit, typically payable in about 30 days. These credit purchases are the accounts payable. Just as the accounts receivable consist of money due from a number of customers, the accounts payable consist of money owed to many vendors and suppliers—thousands in a large firm. Consequently, there is constant activity in the payables process, as maturing accounts are paid and new accounts payable are added. However, even though individual payables usually come and go rather quickly, the total pool of payables provides a constant source of financing (one that grows along with the company). Most firms manage their payables so that they maintain control of these funds for as long as possible without unduly antagonizing their creditors.

Accrued Liabilities

The term *accrued liabilities* (sometimes called *accrued expenses*) refers to expenses for which the benefit has been received but the payment is not yet due. Accrued salaries are a prime example. Employees earn their salaries every day they work, but they are not paid every day. And even on payday, they may not be paid up to that very day. As a result, at the end of the month, some unpaid salary expense usually accrues. This amount is listed on the balance sheet as a liability, along with property taxes, vacation pay, interest, and any other accrued expenses.

Income Taxes

A business pays its estimated income taxes in four installments during the year. The actual taxes are figured at year-end, and any difference between estimated and actual taxes is due within 2½ months of the fiscal year-end.

Long-Term Debt Due Within One Year and Long-Term Debt

Long-term debts extend beyond a year. Most require some type of installment payments, and any amounts due in the next 12 months are listed in the Current Liabilities section of the balance sheet.

Deferred Income Taxes and Other Noncurrent Liabilities

We've already discussed deferred income taxes under "assets." Other noncurrent liabilities might include a provision for employee pensions or bonuses, an estimate of future warranty expense for products already sold, or even a claim that may have to be paid because of a lawsuit.

Equity

Since the common meaning of *equity* is "fairness" or "justice," it may seem like an odd word to describe the shareholders' interest in the corporation. Perhaps *equity* is used because the shareholders get what is left over—good or bad—when the liabilities are subtracted from the assets. And that seems fair. To restate our equation:

$$Assets - liabilities = equity$$

The two major classes of shareholders are *common* and *preferred*. Both classes have a vote in electing directors, and both receive *dividends* from the company's earnings. The holders of *preferred stock* receive the first portion of the dividends—usually a fixed amount. (General Instrument's preferred dividends are $3 per share annually.) The holders of *common stock* receive the remaining earnings. This may sound like bad news, but it isn't; what is left may be quite a large amount. What's more, if the company prospers, common stock dividends are likely to increase, while preferred dividends remain unchanged.

The preferred shareholders are "favored" if the firm is liquidated, either through bankruptcy or voluntary dissolution. They are paid in full for their shares before any funds are paid to the common shareholders. That too may sound like bad news for the common shareholders—and it is. But a liquidation is seldom good news for the preferred shareholders, either. In most bankruptcies, neither group receives anything.

The preferred stock of General Instrument is described as "cumulative convertible preferred stock," which sounds much more confusing than it is. *Cumulative* simply means that if the preferred dividend (in this case, $3) is not paid for one or more years due to insufficient earnings, the company must pay those missed dividends plus the current dividend before the common shareholders receive anything. *Convertible* refers to a special option to exchange preferred shares for common shares. In our example, the notes to the financial statements (which are not shown in Figure 3-1) explain that "each preferred share is convertible to 0.82 shares of common stock." Because investors can convert their preferred stock to take advantage of an increase in the common stock's market price and/or dividends, the convertible feature makes the stock easier to sell.

Note that the preferred stock of General Instrument is "without par value," while the common stock has a par value of $1.00. At one time, *par value* meant the price at which the stock was originally issued. Today it bears no relation to the market value and is usually set at $1.00 or $1.25 because the company must pay a franchise tax that is based on the par value. Because the common stock has a par value of $1.00, a separate account called "additional paid-in capital" is used to show the amount in excess of par value that the company received when the stock was issued.

By the way, most of the buying and selling of shares through stockbrokers is between one investor and another, and the transactions have no direct effect—good or bad—on the company. The balance sheet is affected only when the company buys or sells its own shares.

Retained Earnings

Retained earnings are also called *earned surplus*. When a business earns a profit, part of that money is usually given to the shareholders as dividends, and the rest is plowed back into the company to help finance its growth. The amounts kept in the company are accumulated in the Retained Earnings account and belong to the common shareholders. But don't be confused; retained earnings do *not* constitute a cash fund. They simply represent some unspecified portion of the total assets. (Assets = liabilities + equity. And Equity = issued value of the stock + retained earnings.)

The significance of the items on the balance sheet is discussed further in Chapter 8, "Analyzing Financial Statements."

THE INCOME STATEMENT

The *income statement* (also called *profit and loss statement* and *statement of operations*) lists the sales and expenses of the company and the resulting profit or loss. An "official" income statement is presented once a year, although most large corporations issue interim reports each quarter, and nearly all companies prepare monthly income statements for their internal use. Figure 3-2 shows General Instrument's 1979 and 1980 income statements.

Most American businesses exist on a thin crust of profit—an average of five to six cents of every sales dollar. This slim margin means that a mistake in pricing, a sharp rise in costs, or a drop in sales volume can quickly wipe out the entire profit. If the loss of profit appears to be the

Figure 3-2.   Income statement for General Instrument Corporation.

Consolidated Statement of Income   General Instrument Corporation and Subsidiaries
Years ended February 29, 1980 and February 28, 1979

	1980	1979
Revenue	$718,103,819	$550,648,002
Costs and expenses:		
Cost of sales and services	556,999,507	423,283,331
Selling, general and administrative expenses	64,695,497	58,214,671
Interest income	(6,977,188)	(5,286,942)
Interest expense	5,055,729	7,551,420
	619,773,545	483,762,480
Income before income taxes	98,330,274	66,885,522
Provision for income taxes	47,200,000	32,800,000
Net income	51,130,274	34,085,522
Dividends on preferred stock	1,560,742	1,560,774
Earnings on common stock	$ 49,569,532	$ 32,524,748
Earnings per common share:		
Primary	$5.90	$4.22
Fully diluted	5.41	3.77

result of some fundamental change in the business, such as reduced demand for the product, investors and creditors will begin to lose interest in the company and withdraw their support. The case of Chrysler Corporation is a large-scale example. Because of its doubtful prospects in the late 1970s, the company found it difficult to obtain borrowed or invested money to resuscitate the firm and turned to the government as a lender of last resort.

As powerful as the big corporations appear with their large factories, plush offices, and billions of dollars flowing through their checking accounts annually, their true power lies in their ability to create customers—an ability that is tested afresh each day. The income statement summarizes this ability in money terms.

Revenue

The income statement begins with *revenue,* or "net sales"—the total of all sales minus any returned merchandise. A variety of costs or expenses are then deducted from revenue to arrive at *net income*—the bottom line.

Costs

These costs are listed in the general order of their importance to the basic operations of the business. The first is *cost of sales.* Another term for it—slightly out-of-date but still used—is "cost of goods sold." This older term is more descriptive than cost of sales, but an even better description would be "cost of producing the goods sold," for these are costs directly connected with making or buying the products or providing the services. For a retail store, cost of sales is the wholesale price of the stock in trade. For a manufacturer, it refers to the cost of "direct labor" (production workers), "raw materials" (any parts of the products purchased from outsiders, whether raw, finished, or in-between), and "overhead" (or "burden"—essential but indirect production costs like factory utilities or supervisors' salaries).

Subtracting the cost of sales from net sales or revenue yields *gross profit,* and gross profit as a percentage of sales is the *gross profit rate.* Although General Instrument's income statement doesn't show these figures, we can calculate them. (Figures here are expressed to the nearest million.)

	Years Ended	
	2/29/80	2/28/79
Revenue	$718	$551
Less: Cost of Sales and Service	557	423
Gross Profit	$161	$128
Gross Profit Rate	22%	23%

Selling, General, and Administrative Expenses

Selling, general, and administrative expenses (the last two known as "G & A") are indirect operating costs. That is, they are not vital to the making of the products, but they are necessary for the existence of the organization and the distribution (selling) of its products. In some financial reports, these amounts are deducted from gross profit to arrive at a figure called *operating profit*. For example:

	Years Ended	
	2/29/80	2/28/79
Gross profit	$161	$128
Less: Selling and G&A expenses	65	58
Operating profit	$ 96	$ 70
Operating profit rate (operating profits as a percentage of revenue)	13.4%	12.7%

General Instrument follows the modern trend of not showing a figure for operating profit. Except for internal use in running the company, only the final profit figure really counts. Too often the intermediate profit figures are converted to financial propaganda. If, for example, we wanted to put the best face on the General Instrument report, we might highlight the operating profit rate, which was up this year compared to last year, and list, without comment, the gross profit rate, which declined.

Interest Income and Interest Expense

Interest income and interest expense are often separated from the firm's other earnings and expenses. Unlike other revenues, interest income is not related to the company's ability to sell its product, but to the amount of money it has to invest. Interest expense is considered a discretionary rather than a necessary expense. In theory, a company has the option of financing itself entirely from equity funds (common stock and retained earnings), thus having no interest expense. Therefore, the theory goes, if the company decides to borrow some of the money needed to run the business, the decision is financial, not operational. In practice, entrepreneurs tend to prefer borrowing money to selling more stock, and the interest expense seems to be primarily a function of the opportunity to borrow. This point will be explored further in Chapter 8, when we discuss leverage.

Income Before Income Tax

Income (profit) before tax is another frequently displayed rung on the profit ladder. However, because taxes are a common and necessary expense, many companies list taxes along with other expenses without showing the pretax profit figure.

Net Income

Net income (or *net profit*) is the famous "bottom line," now a cliché even in some nonbusiness activities. It is the final result of perhaps a thousand variables that begin with demand for the product, price, distribution, management, quality of employees, raw materials, supplies, and so on. This all-important figure is the one shareholders use to judge management, the one potential investors project into the future in deciding whether to buy the company's stock, and the one creditors use to measure the risk that they will not be repaid.

Earnings on Common Stock and Earnings Per Common Share

All of a corporation's profits belong to its shareholders. However, when there are preferred stockholders, their fixed dividends are deducted from net income; the remaining profits, or *earnings on common stock,* belong to the common stockholders. These earnings are divided by the number of common shares outstanding (those shares issued and not owned by the company) to give the *earnings per share (EPS).*

The General Instrument income statement gives two EPS figures. *Primary* earnings are the figure we've just described, while the *fully diluted* amount shows the EPS if all convertible preferred stock were to be

Figure 3-3.   Statement of stockholders' equity for General Instrument Corporation.

Consolidated Statement of Stockholders' Equity

	Cumulative Convertible Preferred Stock		Common Stock ($1 Par Value)	Additional Paid-in Capital	Retained Earnings
	Shares	Amount			
Balance March 1, 1978	520,358	$13,008,950	$7,549,760	$71,968,774	$105,210,275
Shares issued:					
Exercise of stock options			236,227	2,704,683	
Income tax benefits resulting from the exercise of nonqualified stock options				864,000	
Conversion of preferred stock	(100)	(2,500)	82	2,418	
Conversion of debentures			34,790	858,369	
Net income					34,085,522
Cash dividends:					
Preferred stock ($3.00 per share)					(1,560,774)
Common stock ($.55 per share)					(4,322,144)
Balance February 28, 1979	520,258	13,006,450	7,820,859	76,398,244	133,412,879
Shares issued:					
Exercise of stock options			101,648	1,616,837	
Income tax benefits resulting from the exercise of nonqualified stock options				886,000	
Conversion of preferred stock	(15)	(375)	12	363	
Conversion of:					
10¼% debentures			710,923	18,492,607	
4¼% debentures			25,223	619,535	
Net income					51,130,274
Cash dividends:					
Preferred stock ($3.00 per share)					(1,560,742)
Common stock ($.75 per share)					(6,402,316)
Balance February 29, 1980	520,243	$13,006,075	$8,658,665	$98,013,586	$176,580,095
See accompanying notes.					

exchanged for common stock. (Remember: the exchange rate is 0.82 share of common stock for one share of preferred.)

Statement of Stockholders' Equity

The statement of stockholders' equity (Figure 3-3), which follows the General Instrument income statement, is a detailed description of the changes in the various equity accounts—that is, how the balance sheet equity figures changed from the beginning to the end of the fiscal year. For example, the "retained earnings" column (far right) shows the addition of profit and the issuing of preferred and common stock dividends.

THE STATEMENT OF CHANGES

The *statement of changes*—or consolidated statement of changes in financial position (Figure 3-4), as it is formally known—is one of those

Figure 3-4. Statement of changes for General Instrument Corporation.

Consolidated Statement of Changes in Financial Position

General Instrument Corporation and Subsidiaries

Years ended February 29, 1980 and February 28, 1979

	1980	1979
Sources of funds:		
From operations:		
Net income	$ 51,130,274	$ 34,085,522
Charges (credits) not affecting working capital:		
Depreciation and amortization	32,364,073	27,124,812
Non-current deferred income taxes	6,623,000	(112,855)
Provisions for long-term liabilities	3,686,000	3,200,000
Equity in net income of GICC	(649,133)	(975,193)
Working capital provided by operations	93,154,214	63,322,286
Stock issued on conversion of debentures, primarily 10¼% debentures in 1980 (see below)	19,848,288	893,159
Receipts from (advances to) GICC	6,832,705	(415,342)
Proceeds from stock options and related income tax benefits	2,604,485	3,804,910
Decrease in long-term receivables	661,817	1,473,367
Increase in long-term debt	252,287	3,666,112
Other, net	186,328	676,818
	123,540,124	73,421,310
Uses of funds:		
Additions to fixed assets, net of dispositions of $1,214,000 and $3,065,000 in 1980 and 1979	80,914,296	43,606,593
Decrease in long-term debt (see above)	20,420,784	2,426,851
Non-current assets of company acquired	8,515,000	
Cash dividends	7,963,058	5,882,918
Current maturities on long-term debt	2,473,346	173,088
	120,286,484	52,089,450
Increase in working capital	$ 3,253,640	$ 21,331,860
Working capital changes-increase (decrease):		
Cash and temporary investments	$ (25,591,126)	$ 23,053,767
Accounts receivable	21,443,334	6,853,096
Inventories	34,536,962	12,377,232
Deferred income taxes and prepaid expenses	7,559,552	846,638
Notes and loans payable	4,133,937	(2,902,017)
Accounts payable	(19,706,106)	(7,929,010)
Accrued liabilities	(12,803,864)	(11,964,137)
Income taxes	(4,269,354)	(13,405,141)
Long-term debt due within one year	(2,049,695)	14,401,432
	$ 3,253,640	$ 21,331,860

See accompanying notes.

curious perversities that sometimes occur when a simple and useful idea is given professional treatment. The idea was to answer the question: How has the company's balance sheet changed in the last year? The answer is useful because companies are continually changing—usually growing—and if some balance sheet items change disproportionately, that may indicate a developing weakness. For example, if the cash balance has declined while accounts payable have increased, the result may be past-due payments to some suppliers.

The format of the statement of changes, however, is an example of professionalism gone astray. The language is stilted, the process of construction convoluted, and the original purpose lost in obscurity. Here we'll discuss only the primary features of the statement of changes.

Sources of Funds

The statement has three main sections. The first is "sources of funds." *Funds* is an ambiguous word that usually means money but may mean money value in some other form. For example, a business acquires funds when it makes a sale; the funds may be either cash or accounts receivable (if the sale is made on credit).

Think of the sources of funds as the business transactions that brought cash into the company. The first source, net income (the "bottom line" from the income statement) is the difference between all the cash that came in from sales and all that went out for expenses. Near the bottom of General Instrument's list of sources is an item labeled "increase in long-term debt." This money came from additional borrowing by the firm.

Uses of Funds

The "uses of funds" section shows where cash was spent—not the ordinary expenses that were accounted for in the net income figure, but less common transactions such as buying new fixtures and equipment (fixed assets) or paying dividends to shareholders.

Changes in Working Capital

The difference between the sources and the uses of funds is the increase (or decrease) in working capital, which is current assets minus current liabilities. In other words, *working capital* is the relatively liquid funds available to the company that are not needed to meet current debts.

Changes in working capital can be shown in two ways. The most obvious way is to total the changes in the current assets and current liabilities accounts, as is done in the third section of General Instrument's statement of changes. And, as we've already seen, subtracting the uses of funds from the sources achieves the same result. Here the report focuses on *how* the changes in working capital occur—changes that involve equity, noncurrent assets, and noncurrent liabilities. For example, if a piece of equipment (a fixed asset) is sold for cash, working capital will increase accordingly because cash is a current asset account. If a long-term note becomes due in less than a year, it becomes a current liability and working capital decreases accordingly. These and all other such transactions either provide funds (serve as sources) or decrease funds through their use.

This is just the barest description of the statement of changes; it won't equip you to understand it fully. But you will remember we started out wanting to know how the balance sheet changed from one year-end to the next. Another way to do that is simply to subtract last year's figure from this year's for each account listed on the balance sheet. This procedure is no less effective than the statement of changes and is considerably easier to do and to understand.

PACKAGING THE DATA:
THE ANNUAL REPORT AND THE 10K

The annual report is one of the tedium-relieving pleasantries of business finance. The regimented lists of figures are often surrounded by photographs, charts, and typography to rival those of many expensive magazines. Of course, the purpose of this costly display is to create a favorable impression of the issuing company—an impression that may or may not be warranted by the financial statements.

The annual report has become an important part of most corporations' public relations effort. This does *not* mean that the information in a report is false or even exaggerated beyond propriety. After all, public relations must be credible to be effective. However, in its report a company presents its best side, and positive thinking abounds. For example, in General Instrument's 1980 report, we learn from the chairman's message on page 2 that sales for the year were 30.4 percent higher than the year before. Very impressive; but on page 35 we see the same figures adjusted to remove the effect of inflation and can calculate a sales increase of 16.4 percent. Both figures are correct and both are quite favorable, but the more impressive one gets top billing.

Most annual reporting has three distinguishable parts. They are as follows:

1. The glossy management message to the stockholders and public, designed more to impress than inform.

2. The financial reports prepared by or with the approval of the firm's certified public accountants. This section includes the income statement, balance sheet, and statement of changes, usually accompanied by several pages of supplementary schedules and footnotes. Though it may seem unexciting, this section is the most useful for appraising the company's financial strength.

3. The annual *10K* report to the *Securities and Exchange Commission (SEC)* required of all companies whose stock is publicly held. The 10K contains the financial reports and additional financial details about management stock options, long-term leases, inventories, and depreciation policies. Unlike the glossy management message, the 10K is written frankly to avoid making things sound better than they are and may even err a little in the other direction. This approach is due in part to the fact that it is necessary for the chief executive officer and chief financial officer of the company to certify that the 10K is correct. They would risk serious penalties—including imprisonment—if they were to file false information.

The 10K is a public document, and anyone may obtain a photocopy of it from the SEC. Many companies will furnish copies on request, just as they do with annual reports. 10K reports are used primarily by securities (investment) analysts who comb the footnotes and special disclosures in hopes of finding some tidbit that might affect the stock market price before anyone else finds it. For commonplace transactions between companies, such detail is unnecessary.

Although most annual reports are of the no-nonsense variety, some refreshing candor or a touch of humor appears now and then. One such occasion reported by *The Wall Street Journal* serves to remind us that money isn't everything.

Annual-report historians still speak wistfully of Cybermatics Inc., a New Jersey graphic-arts concern that used to be in the computer software business. One of the great moments in annual-report history was the arrival of Cybermatics' 1969 report; the tone was set by photos of and comments from "eight impartial observers." The observers included: The cleaning lady ("Trash at Cybermatics is up 630%"); the lunch delivery boy ("They ordered seven times more cheeseburgers than the year before"); the window washer ("They look busier than last year"); and the handyman, pictured cradling eight rolls of toilet paper ("A year ago this was a one-roll-a-week company. Today it's an eight-roll-a-week company").

OTHER MANAGEMENT REPORTS

There are many other kinds of financial reports, most of which are not available to the general public. These internal reports serve a variety of needs or whims, depending on their content. Here are brief descriptions of some of the most common reports.

Financial planning reports, which are discussed at length in Chapters 13 and 14, include budgets, profit plans, and the like.

An *accounts receivable aging* is a list of the amounts customers owe, broken down into columns headed "current," "30 days past due," "60 days past due," and so on. This report makes it easy to select those accounts needing special attention. An *accounts payable aging* analyzes the monies the company owes in the same way.

Expense reports from employees who travel for the company are usually for relatively insignificant amounts of money. But because such reports often arouse feelings of greed, curiosity, or envy, they generally get far more attention than they deserve. It has been said that the income tax and traffic laws have made petty criminals of us all—and if those two don't do it, the expense account will.

Capital budgeting analyses are performed when a company undertakes some new project or faces a sizable replacement cost. Examples include bringing out a new product, opening a sales office in Europe, or buying a new fleet of forklifts. The capital budget analysis is a miniature profit plan for each project. Its purpose is to show whether a given project will add to the company's *rate* of profit (any profit at all will add to the dollar amount, but the ratio of profit to equity might be lowered), or which projects being considered are expected to be the most profitable. Capital budgeting analysis is an important and fairly new management tool; we'll discuss it further in Chapter 11.

Chapter 4

Forms of Business Organization

If you were to list all of the terms used to describe a business organization, you'd find that they fit in two categories: general and technical. The general terms such as *company* are fine for casual conversations or for speaking about businesses in general. The technical terms such as *corporation* are more sharply defined. These terms imply specific kinds of authority and responsibility; they are used in legal documents to designate who does what to whom. Using technical terms improperly can get you into an embarassing situation. But using these words correctly is an easy way to impress people with your business knowledge.

GENERAL TERMS

Among the general terms used to define a business organization are *company, firm, establishment, enterprise,* and *concern.* These terms are so broad that they apply to the whole range of organizations, from one-person businesses to billion-dollar corporations.

Since a *company* is defined as a group of people working together, the term applies to any business organization. Even a one-person business can call itself a company; there are no legal requirements or restrictions on the term.

The word *firm* also applies to any business organization, but it is sometimes used in a narrower sense to mean an unincorporated business of two or more persons, such as a firm of attorneys. *Establishment* is often used the same way as *firm,* but it can also mean one of the locations at which a company conducts its business. The U.S. Census Bureau defines an establishment as any business office, store, or plant. According to this meaning, one large company may have several establishments at various places.

Enterprise can be used to mean any business, but because the term implies taking risks to make a gain, it is seldom used when speaking of a not-for-profit business. From the same French root comes the word *entrepreneur,* which in France means "contractor," but in America applies to any person organizing a business for profit. The term is most frequently used to describe small businesses and also suggests a willingness to take risks.

The noun *concern* also means any business. Accountants sometimes speak of a "going concern," meaning a continuing business. However, the term is a bit old-fashioned. Today if you speak of a "business concern," people may think you are referring to some worry or anxiety about the business.

TECHNICAL TERMS

The technical terms discussed below should be used with care when describing a business organization. If you are uncertain as to which technical term correctly describes a particular business, use a general term instead. Otherwise, you might mislead or confuse someone.

Proprietorship

A *proprietorship* (also known as a *sole proprietorship*) is an unincorporated business with a single owner. Although *proprietorship* is the more frequently used term, government agencies such as the Internal Revenue Service use the term *sole proprietorship*. Proprietorships are the oldest and most common form of business. The more than 11 million proprietorships in the United States amount to 78 percent of all business enterprises. However, most of these businesses are small, and the dollar amount of sales produced by all of them is only 9 percent of the total for the United States.

Proprietorships are easy to form. Although the paperwork requirements vary somewhat from area to area, they're usually relatively simple. Some cities require you to buy a business license. If you're calling your business by something other than your own name, you'll have to register that fact with the appropriate state or county office. And that's it, unless you're operating a restaurant or other business with special health and building code requirements.

As a proprietorship, you don't have to show anyone a financial statement. You don't even have to prepare one, although it's certainly sound financial management to do so. Also, there's no minimum amount of money needed to form the business.

Proprietorships are so easy to form because they're considered an extension of the persons who own them. Consequently, the owner bears full responsibility for the business's actions. Probably the biggest drawback to a proprietorship is that the owner is personally liable for business debts or the settlement of lawsuits against the business. As a result, the owner's personal assets, such as his or her home or car, may be vulnerable to a claim on the business.

Proprietorships are relatively free from government control. That advantage is really more a function of their size than their business form. If the business has no employees, official formalities amount to little more than an extra schedule you submit with your income tax form detailing the profit or loss from the business, and perhaps the remittance of sales tax. If the business has employees, then you'll have to contend with withholding tax, Social Security, and so forth.

Raising capital for a proprietorship can be either easier or more difficult than with other business forms. New companies almost always have difficulty borrowing money, but a new proprietor may be able to borrow on his or her personal creditworthiness and thus obtain credit when a new corporation couldn't. However, because it is based on the owner's financial condition, the amount of credit available is limited by his or her personal wealth.

The owner's personal liability and the limited availability of capital are usually compelling reasons for incorporating a business once it reaches a significant size.

Partnership

A *partnership* is an unincorporated business owned by two or more people. Partnerships are not a widespread form of business—they account for less than 5 percent of total sales in the United States—but they dominate some important segments of commerce. Most law firms, accounting firms, and stockbrokers are partnerships.

A partnership is easily formed by two or more people joining together in a common enterprise. Typically, a written partnership agreement is drawn up, setting forth the duties and responsibilities of each partner and explaining how the profits and losses are to be divided. The legal requirements are about the same as for a proprietorship.

One of the advantages of a partnership is that it allows pooling of various kinds of resources. One partner may be inventive but have very little money. Another may have the funds but little ingenuity. Each contributes according to his or her abilities, and all share in the profits.

The chancy aspect of a partnership is that all partners are personally liable for the actions of the business, no matter which partner caused the actions. Moreover, each partner is responsible for 100 percent of the liabilities, regardless of his or her share of the business. If a six-person partnership were to go bankrupt and only one partner had any money, that person would be called on to pay all of the debts.

Business partnerships, therefore, require a high degree of trust and respect among the partners. Perhaps that's why in 1494, Italian mathematician Luca Pacioli wrote in the first accounting text: "Books should be closed each year, especially in a partnership, because frequent accounting makes for long friendship."

Partnerships are somewhat tenuous. If one person dies or wants to withdraw from the firm, the partnership is automatically dissolved. If the business is to continue, a new partnership must be formed. In addition, one partner cannot sell or give his or her interest to another partner without the consent of all members of the partnership. Clearly, the partners must be able to work together harmoniously if the arrangement is to continue for very long.

One of the limitations of a partnership is its restricted ability to raise capital. The partnership can't give investors a share of the profits without making them partners. Also, the amount of money it can borrow is dependent on the partners' investment (which may be modest) and on their personal creditworthiness. Because of these considerations, all states have now enacted legislation permitting a variation called a "limited partnership," which allows more freedom in attracting capital.

Limited Partnership

A *limited partnership* permits some partners a limited liability. With this variation, the partnership has at least one general partner with unlimited liability and one or more limited partners. A limited partner invests

in the business and shares in the profits and losses, but has no voice in
the management of the business. The liability of such a partner is limited
to the amount of his or her investment.

Corporation

A *corporation* is an organization formed by a group of shareholders
and endowed by state law with the right to act as a legal entity or person.
Just like an individual, a corporation can own property, employ workers,
and borrow money. The chief advantage of the corporate form is that the
liability of the shareholders (or stockholders) is limited to the amount of
their investment. What's more, new shareholders can come in and old
ones can leave without interrupting the business or disturbing the agreements made by the corporation.

This characteristic of limited liability permits the business to seek
capital from many different people. Investors are willing to become
shareholders in a company which they may never have seen and which is
managed by people they've never met because they know they're risking
only the money they invest. If the corporation goes bankrupt, their personal assets won't be in jeopardy. And, of course, there is the hope of
substantial gain if the corporation flourishes. Moreover, a corporation's
willingness to divide the capital into many shares makes it attractive to
small investors as well as large.

An easy mistake to make if you're dealing with small corporations
is the failure to distinguish between corporate wealth and the personal wealth
of the investors. A multimillionaire may form a corporation with an investment of $10,000. He or she may even be president of the firm. But
any transactions you make with the company should rely only on the corporate wealth. The owner's personal millions are protected by the corporate armor of limited liability.

Among the disadvantages of the corporate form are the expense and
bother of getting a corporate charter. Compounding this drawback is the
fact that additional paperwork and fees are usually needed to operate in
states other than the one that issued the original charter. Another disadvantage is that corporate profits are taxed twice. First, the corporation pays
taxes of up to 46 percent on its income. Then when the earnings are paid
to the shareholders as dividends, the shareholders must report them as
income and pay taxes accordingly. Corporations are also subject to heavy
government regulation.

One example of such regulations is the intricate rules of the *Securities and Exchange Commission (SEC)*. The SEC's unremitting vigilance
and sharp bite have made most corporations paragons of virtue when dealing

with their shareholders. As a result, potential investors have accurate information to use when evaluating the stock. This aspect of regulation works to the corporation's advantage as well as the shareholders', because when people have confidence in the validity of the financial statements, they are more likely to invest.

One probably unavoidable disadvantage of the modern corporation is the lack of control shareholders have over management. Theoretically, shareholders have a voice in the running of the business through the directors whom they elect. But as a practical matter, the ownership of most large corporations is so diverse that shareholders have little power unless they act together, and they usually have little inclination or ability to do so. In some cases, they may show their dissatisfaction through spirited comments and questions at the annual stockholders' meeting. Such dialogues are usually the only interesting aspect of these meetings. But most unhappy shareholders simply sell their stock.

Thus, while the corporation's ownership is democratic, its management is relatively autocratic. This concentration of enormous power in the hands of a few persons can create major corporate successes and equally substantial failures. At times this power is abused, as when less-than-competent executives use their power to extend their stay in office. Through their influence in nominating directors and picking subordinates and successors, they can protect their policies and interests from attack by unhappy shareholders.

However, the solution is not simply giving shareholders more power. Getting thousands of shareholders to agree on an appropriate course of action is virtually impossible. Besides, the shareholders' prime interest is usually more profit for themselves. While corporations should be concerned about that, too, they must also consider their responsibilities to their customers, their employees, and the public. It's difficult to be fair to all parties, and some companies try harder at it than others.

Other Forms of Business Organization

Proprietorships, partnerships, and corporations are the major types of business. However, you should also be familiar with the following other forms.

A *joint venture* is a partnership or corporation formed to carry out a particular project. This situation usually occurs when the project is too large for one firm alone or when there is a fortuitous combination of resources among the participants. Although a joint venture may be a permanent arrangement, often there are provisions for one partner to buy out the other(s) after a certain time period. Some examples of joint ventures are: an oil company joining with a coal producer to manufacture a new synthetic material; two large construction companies pooling resources to build a dam in Egypt; and a department store and a local real estate developer combining a build a shopping center.

A *subsidiary* is a corporation all or a majority of whose stock is owned by another corporation, called the "parent." When the parent owns all of the stock, the subsidiary is referred to as "wholly owned." The parent may form a subsidiary in order to carry on a specialized business, as when Montgomery Ward & Company, Inc., formed the Montgomery Ward Insurance Company to sell life insurance. Subsidiaries may also result from a merger or acquisition, as when the Mobil Corporation acquired the majority stock of Montgomery Ward.

Eventually, a complex "family tree" of parents and subsidiaries may be formed. In the above example, Mobil is the parent of Montgomery Ward, which is itself the parent of Montgomery Ward Insurance Company; and the chain could continue further.

A common supposition in business is that a parent corporation will underwrite a subsidiary's obligations. In reality, a parent will support a subsidiary only as long as the subsidiary doesn't threaten the parent's own survival. Corporate shareholders have limited liability, just as individual shareholders do. If a subsidiary gets into serious enough trouble, the parent may decide to let it go bankrupt—despite the loss of reputation—rather than throw good money after bad.

As a less drastic resort, a parent may sell a troubled subsidiary either to another corporation or to a qualified group of investors. For example, the subsidiary's management or employees may decide to buy it and run it as they see fit. Often such sales result in a healthier parent and a successful new company. Just as in life, some corporate "marriages" do not work out, and the parties involved function better separately.

A *division* is usually a major segment of a corporation, not a separate entity. A division has no legal existence of its own but is merely a convenient internal partition. For example, the publisher of this book, AMACOM, is one of several divisions of the American Management Associations. Any obligations contracted by a division are obligations of the corporation.

Affiliates are companies in some way associated with each other. The association may take the form of a subsidiary–parent relationship, a joint venture, or something less direct, such as two corporations with the same stockholders. *Affiliate* is one of those general terms that does not describe the legal status of the association.

A *not-for-profit corporation* is formed to carry on educational, humanitarian, or charitable activities. Such corporations are usually founded by grants or contributions and directed by a designated group of trustees. Like profit-making corporations, not-for-profit ones must be licensed in a particular state and must meet a variety of legal and regulatory requirements designed to ensure their legitimacy. Not-for-profit corporations pay no income tax because they are not supposed to have any income. However, these organizations are legally allowed to retain a small percentage of earnings "in excess of expenses." This amount is not profit and does provide a small cushion if times become difficult.

Chapter 5

Taking GAAS and Bridging the GAAP: Accounting Standards and Principles

No, we didn't make up GAAS or even GAAP. They are two of the most basic accounting acronyms. GAAP stands for *generally accepted accounting principles*. These are the rules that accountants, particularly certified public accountants (see Chapter 6), follow. These rules have been developed over 600 years of accounting practice; they have been adopted by the *American Institute of Certified Public Accountants (AICPA)*, a professional organization that influences CPAs much as the American Medical Association does doctors.

The second acronym, GAAS, means *generally accepted auditing standards*. The AICPA issued these rules to guide its members when they review financial statements for accuracy. The CPA members, which include virtually all large accounting firms, are required to follow these rules and procedures when they audit a client company's books and records.

If you look at the annual report for a company whose financial statements have been audited by a CPA, you'll find a letter signed by the CPA firm—the auditor's opinion. This letter usually says that the CPAs have examined the statements in accordance with GAAS and have found that they conform to GAAP—about as nice a compliment as you can pay a financial statement. However, if the company did not follow GAAP, that fact will be stated. Likewise, if the auditors feel the company may not be able to continue operations, they'll disclose their doubts.

Now, you might think the phrase "generally accepted" implies fence straddling. But in practice there is little question among accountants as to what constitutes GAAP. Even though these principles have developed informally over many years, they have become thoroughly established through their widespread use. Of course, new ones are continually being formulated to cope with new circumstances such as inflation, changes in tax regulations, and new forms of business (franchising, for example). When old principles come to seem inappropriate, accountants try new techniques. If these techniques result in fairer and more accurate financial statements, new principles gradually emerge.

Before we discuss the most important GAAP, you should become familiar with two other acronyms: APB and FASB. To police and felons, an APB is an "all points bulletin"; to accountants, it's the *Accounting Principles Board*. The accounting profession established the APB in 1960 in a move to formalize the development of new principles. The APB issued many "opinions" and "exposure drafts" (tentative opinions) which the vast majority of accountants adopted.

In 1973, the APB was succeeded by the *Financial Accounting Standards Board* (FASB). The FASB is a standing committee, financed by the CPAs but supposedly independent. It reviews accounting problem situations and through a lengthy process formulates and issues "statements" which become part of GAAP. The FASB consists of 7 teaching accountants and a professional staff of over 100. And they are prolific: recently, the volume of rules increased by 13 percent in one year. The FASB's statement on leasing alone is over 225 pages. Many accountants are beginning to question the need for such detailed statements, given the high cost of attempting to comply. (Now you see one reason that accounting departments keep getting larger!)

But relax—interpreting FASB statements is your accounting department's problem, not yours. You should, however, be familiar with some of the more important accounting principles. These will help you understand your accountants' decisions.

THE GOING-CONCERN PRINCIPLE

Unless there is evidence to the contrary, it is assumed that a business is a *going concern*—that is, it will continue indefinitely into the future. This assumption arises from two circumstances: (1) one of the accountant's most important tasks is reporting the ''true'' profits of a business each year, and (2) many assets last more than one year, so an annual valuation is required in order to obtain a ''true'' profit figure.

For example, if a company buys a small truck for $20,000 and expects that truck to last five years, it is reasonable to divide the $20,000 into five parts and to deduct—or ''write off''—one part from the profits of each of those years. That procedure will give a truer picture of yearly profits than deducting the whole cost in the year the money was spent. But the profits will really be true only if the company lasts five years or if the truck can be sold for the balance of the cost yet to be expensed.

The going-concern principle permits the orderly writeoff of assets over a period of time. Without that assumption, the assets' value would be their worth at a quick sale, which often isn't much: one study showed that the amounts received in bankruptcy sales, as compared to the undepreciated costs of the assets involved, averaged only 9 cents on the dollar. Consequently, financial statements prepared on a ''liquidation'' basis would present a very bleak and unrealistic picture for a ''going concern.'' Of course, if the company were to be liquidated, the financial statements would be prepared accordingly.

THE ACCOUNTING-PERIOD PRINCIPLE

Although most commerce flows in a continuous stream of transactions, accountants arbitrarily measure the flow in yearly segments—the traditional accounting period. The results of the year's activities are then presented in annual financial statements. This annual measurement is now a necessity, as well as a tradition, because tax and securities laws require annual reporting.

This preoccupation with precise 12-month periods sometimes results in a distorted view of a company's performance. A firm usually grows in fits and starts. If the company is in a temporary decline at the accounting cutoff period, the financial statements may deceptively signal a setback. Moreover, many managers are beset by a need to show unbroken yearly increases in sales or profits. To create these increases, they may order a year-end delay or speed-up of production, shipments, or purchases. Such wrenching of transactions to make them fit into a smooth growth curve results from short-term thinking—placing excessive emphasis on immediate results as opposed to long-term growth.

Besides annual reports, most companies prepare interim unaudited statements—quarterly for shareholders and monthly for management. Some firms—department stores, for example—like to compare the same weeks from year to year. Their annual reports may cover 52 weeks (53 every fifth year or so), and instead of monthly interim reports, they may prepare financial statements on an alternating 4-4-5–week basis.

THE REALIZATION OF REVENUE

This next principle may sound a little strange at first: revenues are generally recorded, or realized, when the sale is made (that is, when the goods are delivered or the services rendered). The timing of the customer's actual payment does not affect this realization of revenue. At the time of sale, the earning process is complete, and your company is entitled to the revenue. Consequently, the accounting department records it at that time. (In the next section, you'll see how the system accounts for the customer who doesn't pay.)

You'll notice we used our old friend "generally" in stating the principle of realization. That's because there are exceptions to this one. Companies mining precious metals sometime recognize them as revenue when they're mined, on the theory that these metals are as negotiable as cash. Likewise, agricultural commodities are sometimes recognized as revenue when they are harvested because their price and sale are assured by government support programs. For major construction projects, revenue may be recognized on a percentage-of-completion basis. This means that the revenue and costs are recognized each year in proportion to the amount of work done.

MATCHING OF EXPENSES

Just as realization determines when revenues will be recorded, matching determines when expenses will be recorded. The *matching* principle holds that all expenses that relate to or "match up" with the revenues of a given year are deducted from those revenues, even though the expenses may actually be paid in another year. This matching of expenses to revenues is essential for determining the business's profits or losses.

Either directly or indirectly, expenses in business should produce revenues (sales). But occasionally there is a time gap between the two events. If we manufacture a product in November 1983 and sell it in January 1984, we want to deduct the manufacturing expense from 1984 sales. If, instead, we deduct the expense from 1983 sales, we understate the 1983 profits and overstate those of 1984. Therefore, our accountants will defer the accounting for the manufacturing expense (not the payment) until the product is sold.

If the revenue is recognized before the expense, matching still occurs. For example, the company's 1983 credit sales are bound to result in some losses due to bad debts. That bad-debt expense is clearly related to 1983 sales, but we may not be aware of the full amount until mid-1984 or even later—long after the 1983 profits have been calculated. Therefore, at the end of 1983, the company *estimates* the eventual bad-debt expense arising from 1983 sales. The estimated amount is then deducted from 1983 revenues under the principle of matching revenues and expenses.

Matching and realization are the foundations of *accrual accounting*. As you might expect, the accrual method of accounting recognizes revenues and their related expenses when they occur, and not necessarily when the money changes hands. The accrual method's opposite is *cash accounting,* in which transactions are recorded at the time cash is received or paid out. Cash accounting is not according to GAAP and is used primarily by very small, unincorporated businesses.

HISTORICAL COST

As we mentioned in Chapter 3, the firm's fixed assets—its property, plant, and equipment—are listed on the balance sheet at the prices paid when the assets were bought, or at their *historical cost*. The depreciation of assets is also based on their historical cost.

Although historical cost is definitely part of GAAP, there is a problem. The values shown ignore the effects of inflation and tell nothing about the current worth of the assets or what it would cost to replace them. It's not that accountants don't want to include current values on the balance sheet; it's just that they haven't found a really reliable way to do it.

You can appreciate their dilemma if you ask yourself what your home (or other piece of property) is worth today. You know what it *was* worth when you bought it. But what it's worth today is only your guess, and guesses on costly assets can be miles apart, even when experts are doing the guessing. For example, the *Buena Park* (California) *News* recently reported on the Buena Park School District's proposed sale of a building to the City of Buena Park:

> The city . . . recently received a price of $1.6 million for the property from independent appraiser Donahue and Company of Santa Ana. The school district also received an appraisal, $2.7 million, from American Appraisal Associates. That's only a $1,100,000 difference.

So the accounting profession has some justification for opposing the use of appraisals and estimates on the balance sheet, but the problem of unrealistic historical costs remains.

For now, the compromise is FASB Statement No. 33. This rule requires annual reports of large corporations to include supplemental tables which show the current cost of assets and which convert earnings and expenses into "constant dollars." In other words, the original amounts are adjusted in an attempt to eliminate the effect of inflation. FASB 33 is an "off the balance sheet" way of coping with the problem. No one feels that it's a final answer, but it is a step toward a solution.

MATERIALITY

Another important accounting principle is that of *materiality*. Financial reporting is concerned only with significant, or material, information. To put it another way, accountants aren't the nitpickers you may have thought they were.

One example of materiality is the treatment of relatively inexpensive assets as expenses. As you'll remember from Chapter 2, what distinguishes an asset from an expense is how long the item will last. If it will last less than a year, as a box of typewriter ribbons does, then it is an expense in the year purchased. But if the item lasts longer than a year, as a typewriter does, it is classified as an asset and its cost is depreciated.

Now, what about a $25 calculator? Since it should last over a year, technically it's an asset. By that logic, it should be added to the list of equipment and depreciated. But CPAs aren't *that* picky. When an expenditure is immaterial to the overall profit picture, GAAP allow it to be accounted for in the most convenient way. So the calculator will be written off as an expense at the time it's purchased.

Companies set their own limits on what will be expensed as immaterial. Key considerations are the reactions of their outside accountants and the IRS, their internal controls, the increased accounting expense that results when an item is depreciated, and the size of the firm. Most companies pick a figure between $200 and $2,000; any purchase under that amount is considered an expense.

The principle of materiality is also applied in order to determine whether or not an amount is significant enough to be disclosed separately in the financial statements. For example, if research and development expenditures are immaterial, they would be lumped together with other selling and G&A expenses in the annual report. Again, the criterion for materiality varies from firm to firm, but it's usually any amount that represents 3 to 5 percent of the total.

CONSERVATISM

Conservatism here refers not to the accountants' clothing or political views, but to the cautious attitude they are required to take toward items on the financial statements. This attitude counterbalances the optimism that businesspeople usually have about the company's prospects, which may lead them to overstate values and to minimize problems on the financial statements. The principle of conservatism holds that the measurement of assets and income should tend toward understatement rather than overstatement. To put it another way, recognize your losses when they appear likely, but record your gains only when they are realized. For example, while the company may think that all accounts receivable will be collected, the CPA is certain that all will not. Or while the company may think that last year's model can be sold at full price, the accountant will be skeptical and will probably require a writedown of some inventory values. Likewise, the accountant doesn't care if your land has tripled in value until you sell it and actually reap the profits.

Accounting conservatism peaked in the 1920s and 1930s, when some banks were persuaded to write down the value of their opulent head offices to a nominal $1. But in recent years accountants have become less extreme in their conservatism. They now realize that the value of protecting the public with conservative financial statements can sometimes lead to errors of pessimism, as when investors are persuaded to dump a stock because of understated earnings.

FULL DISCLOSURE

Financial statements must not mislead the reader; instead, *full disclosure* of all relevant information is required. One result of this commitment to truthfulness in financial reporting has been the expansion of the footnotes to the financial statements. These footnotes elaborate on, explain, and justify the values on those statements. At times, they're so lengthy that the tail seems to wag the dog. One recent annual report audited by a Big Eight accounting firm offered this 46-word sentence in a footnote:

The assets and obligations for stores leased under capital leases which are closed prior to lease expiration are eliminated from the accounts as of the date of closing and an accrual is provided for anticipated costs to be incurred upon the ultimate disposition of the facility.

This occasional use of stilted, wordy language and jargon is an area in which accountants—like lawyers—can be faulted. However, in most cases full disclosure results in highly professional financial statements in which readers can place a considerable degree of confidence.

Full disclosure also means describing significant events that occurred after the statement date but before the report was published. Here's an example taken from the February 28, 1981, annual report of The Great Atlantic and Pacific Tea Company (the A&P):

Subsequent Event (unaudited)—On April 21, 1981, the Company announced it had reached an agreement in principle to acquire Niagara Frontier Services, Inc., a Buffalo, New York, based operator and franchiser of supermarkets and convenience food outlets. The terms of the acquisition, which are subject to approval by various parties, provide for the purchase of the Niagara shares for approximately $80 million in cash and notes or debentures.

The value of truthful financial statements is difficult to overstate. Just 150 years ago financial statements could not be trusted unless you were convinced of the good "character" of the issuer. Needless to say, this limited the number of business transactions. One result of the safeguards that the government and the accounting profession have imposed on financial statements has been an enormous expansion of commerce. Virtue can be its own reward.

Chapter 6

Audits and CPAs

Accountants can be grouped into two categories: public and private. Private accountants (also called management accountants) are the full-time employees of particular businesses. We've already discussed their role in Chapter 2. Public accountants work on a fee basis, providing accounting services as they are needed.

Public accountants are licensed by the state they operate in and are known as *certified public accountants* (CPAs). To become a CPA, the candidate must pass a rigorous examination given by the American Institute of Certified Public Accountants (AICPA). In most states the candidate is also required to have public accounting experience; the amount of experience necessary varies from one to five years, depending on state law and on the candidate's educational background.

CPA firms range in size from one-person operations to the largest public accounting firms, known as the *Big Eight:* Arthur Andersen; Arthur Young; Coopers and Lybrand; Deloitte Haskins & Sells; Ernst & Whinney; Peat, Marwick, Mitchell; Price Waterhouse; and Touche Ross. Major corporations almost always engage a Big Eight firm to do their public accounting, not only because these firms, with their hundreds of employees, are large enough to handle all their needs but also because prestige is associated with use of these firms.

THE CPA AUDIT

Whatever a CPA firm's size, it serves the same unique function in business: performing an *audit* to verify the accuracy of the organization's financial statements. This public verification enables companies to borrow money from the bank, to buy merchandise on credit from suppliers, and to attract investment funds from individuals all over the country.

The CPA audit also assures management and the board of directors that the values shown on the financial reports are in fact as stated. The larger a business is and the more complex its operations are, the greater the opportunity for mistakes and fraud to pass unnoticed. The knowledge that the books will be audited is a strong incentive for accurate, honest record keeping.

A CPA audit is not a requirement for being in business. When a company is young or small, it usually does without an audit, although it may employ a CPA to help set up the books, to prepare *unaudited* financial statements, and to provide financial and tax advice. Once the business begins to grow and to use more OPM ("other people's money"), the usefulness of the audit becomes increasingly apparent. In fact, lenders such as banks may insist on it.

In addition, an audited financial statement is a badge of honor—a sign that a firm is in "the big leagues." And if the company sells its stock to the public, either through a stock exchange or in the over-the-counter market, the Securities and Exchange Commission (SEC) requires it to have a CPA audit.

WHAT AUDITORS TEST

The CPA audit includes an examination of the company's accounting records and the work done by its accountants. In a smaller firm, the CPA may also help prepare some of these records and reports, but, in general, CPAs are too expensive to hire for routine bookkeeping.

In reviewing a firm's books and records, the CPAs will make "such tests . . . as [are] considered necessary" to verify the accuracy of the financial statements. (This phrasing is standard in all unqualified opinions prepared by CPA firms to accompany financial statements.) Sometimes the client company and the CPA firm will disagree as to what is necessary, but since the client needs the CPAs' good opinion, the CPAs usually win the argument. In fact, if the client interferes with the audit or refuses to pay for sufficient testing, the CPAs must note that fact in their written opinion of the financial statements—which, of course, tends to negate the good opinion that is of such value to the client.

The tests made by the CPAs are concerned more with accounting systems than with accounting records. For example, in examining the company's cash receipts, the auditors seldom bother to doublecheck the amounts or totals on the bank deposit slips. However, they will verify that the person who opens the mail and lists incoming checks is not the same person who prepares the deposit slips. (One of the best deterrents to embezzlement is a system that requires the collaboration of two or more people for fraud.)

Besides examining a company's accounting systems, the auditors will test them a few times to make sure they work as intended. In the above example, the CPAs would randomly pick out several days' lists of checks received and compare them with the deposit slips to verify that every check that came in found its way into the bank account.

The auditors also usually want to witness the taking of inventory. This test of the system is not to verify each quantity but to see that the items counted are tagged so as not to be counted twice and that the people who keep the inventory records are not the same ones who count the items. The CPAs will also test the accounts receivable by asking selected customers—all of the large ones plus a sample of the smaller ones—to verify how much they owe. The inventory and receivables tests are always made when those items represent significant dollar amounts on the balance sheet.

As business systems become more sophisticated, so too do the audits. In recent years CPAs have had to scramble to devise new tests for computer-kept records. The massive computer frauds that occasionally make the headlines remind us that auditing procedures must continually change with the times.

THE CPA FIRM'S WRITTEN OPINION

The findings of a CPA audit are expressed formally in a written opinion that accompanies the client company's financial statements. The opinion may take any of three forms: unqualified, qualified, and "no opinion."

The Unqualified Opinion

An example of a "clean," or unqualified, opinion is shown in Figure 6-1. The stiff, formal phrasing is standard, regardless of the client and the CPA firm. Note, too, that the CPA firm's name is signed rather than an individual's (a partner in the firm does the actual signing). This

Figure 6-1.   Sample unqualified written opinion.

Report of Independent Accountants

To the Board of Directors and Stockholders
of Sanders Associates, Inc.

In our opinion, the accompanying consolidated
balance sheets and the related consolidated
statements of income, stockholders' equity and
changes in financial position present fairly the
financial position of Sanders Associates, Inc. and its
subsidiaries at July 25, 1980 and July 27, 1979, and
the results of their operations and the changes in
their financial position for the years then ended, in
conformity with generally accepted accounting
principles consistently applied. Our examinations
of these statements were made in accordance
with generally accepted auditing standards and
accordingly included such tests of the accounting
records and such other auditing procedures as we
considered necessary in the circumstances.

Price Waterhouse & Co.

Boston, Massachusetts
August 28, 1980

indicates that the CPA firm as a whole accepts responsibility for the opinion.

The three phrases that we've underlined in the opinion deserve a closer inspection.

The first of these is "present fairly." While accountants would prefer to be "accurate" or "factual" rather than "fair," the very nature of accounting frequently allows for more than one legitimate viewpoint. Thus the CPAs say only that the company decided "fairly" in presenting information in its financial statements. For example, suppose we owned a boutique that at year-end had an inventory of goods with a value of $4,000, according to invoices from our suppliers. But if we were forced to sell our goods in a hurry—perhaps because our lease wasn't renewed—we might only realize $2,000. However, our CPA would allow us to use the $4,000 figure because (unless there is contrary evidence) it is "fair" to assume that we will continue in business as a going concern and will eventually realize the full value of the inventory.

Our second key phrase, "generally accepted accounting principles," emphasizes that the client company's financial statements conform to the principles we discussed in Chapter 5. As you'll remember, GAAP are universally followed by the accounting profession and provide a common framework for presenting financial data. When two or more principles conflict, the company's management—not the CPAs—determine which principle will be followed. For example, accrual accounting says that any item purchased for the business that will last more than one year should be classified as an asset and depreciated accordingly. But the principle of materiality allows you to treat an item as an expense rather than an asset if it "doesn't cost too much." Management defines what "doesn't cost too much," and the auditors then determine whether management's decision is fair. While GAAP are followed closely, a CPA can depart from them in exceptional circumstances. For example, according to the AICPA Code of Professional Ethics, an exception may be made when "the financial statements would otherwise have been misleading."

The third significant phrase in the auditors' opinion is "consistently applied." This phrase refers not to consistency throughout the business or among all of the subsidiaries, but to consistency with last year's financial statements. The changes in a balance sheet from year to year are meaningful only if the same accounting methods are used in both years. Thus a company cannot change its method of valuing its inventory unless it fully discloses the change and states the financial effect of the change on the balance sheet.

The Qualified Opinion

While the majority of auditors' opinions are "clean," at times the CPAs must give a qualified opinion. The phrases "subject to" and "except for" in a written opinion signal the auditors' qualification.

A "subject to" opinion is used when an unresolved situation exists that may significantly affect the financial statements. A typical example is a pending lawsuit which, if resolved unfavorably, would materially affect the company's financial position. The suit should be discussed in a footnote to the financial statements, and the auditors should refer to that footnote in their written opinion.

The "except for" clause is used in cases where the company does not conform to a generally accepted accounting principle. Figure 6-2 shows an extract of an opinion letter which mentions an exception to the principle of consistency. (The underscoring is ours.)

If several aspects of the statements do not conform with GAAP, the CPA firm will give an adverse opinion indicating it cannot endorse the statements. Also, if the auditors feel there is a strong possibility that the firm may not be a going concern, they will say so in their opinion. Braniff Airlines, for example, had such an opinion prior to its demise in 1982.

The "No Opinion" Opinion

Smaller firms often call in an outside CPA to do the complicated year-end closing entries on their books and to prepare their financial statements, but not to do the expensive auditing and verification procedures. In an accompanying letter, the CPA firm may describe what it has done and then, in a disclaimer, say that because its efforts were so lim-

Figure 6-2.   "Except for" clause of a written opinion.

In our opinion, the consolidated financial statements referred to above present fairly the financial position of Best Products Co., Inc. and subsidiaries at June 28, 1980 and June 30, 1979, and the results of their operations and the changes in their financial position for the years then ended in conformity with generally accepted accounting principles which, except for the change in the method of valuing merchandise inventories as described on page 13 and with which we concur, were applied on a consistent basis.

Touche Rose + Co.

Richmond, Virginia
August 25, 1980   Certified public accountants

ited, it is unable to express an opinion about the values presented in the financial statements. Here is the way one CPA firm, Kurosaki and Konoshita, Accountants, puts it:

The accompanying [financial statements] have been compiled by us. A compilation is limited to presenting in the form of financial statements information that is the representation of management. We have not audited or reviewed the accompanying financial statements and, accordingly, do not express an opinion or any form of assurance on them.

THE REVIEW

In recent years, CPAs came to realize that the "all or nothing" choices of audited or unaudited financial statements were causing them to miss out on some good business. So they created a third, or middle-ground, option: the review.

A review consists mainly of interviews with company people and analytical tests of the financial data. The work is substantially less than that done in an audit but is sufficient to allow the CPA firm to state whether or not it is aware of any material modifications that should be made to the financial statements. The review is less expensive than an audit but frequently sufficient to satisfy company creditors and other third parties interested in the financial statements.

THE EXTENT OF A CPA'S RESPONSIBILITY

Opinions vary as to the extent of a CPA's responsibility for the financial statements he or she audits. Some people view the outside accountant as just another hired professional—responsible to the client first and to anyone else second. Others want the CPA to act as a watchdog for the public and a guardian of business morality. Most CPA's opinions fall somewhere between these two extremes.

Because of their unique access to corporate data, auditors are under pressure to take an active role in preventing, or at least reporting, business misbehavior. The flaws in their performance in this role were revealed in a series of sensational bankruptcies in the 1960s. The sudden default of Penn Central, the ignominious failure of National Student Marketing, the elaborate fraud of Equity Funding—all pointed up weaknesses in the auditing procedures of the top accounting firms. During the 1970s, it was revealed that CPAs had done little to discover or expose the bribery that was a standard practice for some American firms selling to foreign governments.

Some of these problems are due to the nature of modern business. It takes a well-staffed accounting firm to audit a company with facilities, employees, customers, and bank accounts in several countries. It takes both courage and solid facts to stand up to a client who may be paying a million-dollar fee. And it takes people with experience and knowledge about each business to do an effective job; a good many auditing errors can be attributed to unfamiliarity with company or industry practices.

In 1977 the accounting profession took steps to clarify the auditors' role in dealing with illegal—or seemingly illegal—acts by their clients. The AICPA issued standards that require CPAs to get management's explanation of any suspected illegal act. If such an act isn't accounted for or disclosed in the financial report, the auditors must note it in their opinion letter or, in extreme cases, withdraw from the job and consult their own attorney about further action.

Although auditing failures capture public attention, you should remember that the vast majority of audits are performed in a thorough and professional manner. With a few exceptions, audited financial statements present highly useful and reliable information.

PART TWO

Financial Analysis

Chapter 7

How Tax Strategies Affect Financial Statements

Tax strategies are a major topic of conversation in the finance departments of most businesses. Since finance and accounting personnel don't create or sell products or services, when they receive praise, it's often because they have saved the company money through their tax strategy. Reducing taxes is important, but sometimes it occupies so much of top management's thinking that they neglect their most important mission: to generate profits by offering products and services that customers can use.

With that caveat in mind, we will use this chapter to discuss the more popular legal ways to avoid, minimize, or defer corporate taxes. Some of these strategies result in financial statements that are less than totally realistic. Consequently, you need to be aware of these distortions when you analyze such statements.

CORPORATE INCOME TAXES

By far the largest tax burden for a healthy business is the corporate income tax. This tax, like its counterpart for individuals, is based on earnings, but there are important differences between the two.

The income of a business comes from its revenues or sales, but the business is allowed to deduct all of the expenses involved in generating those revenues. Individuals, in contrast, cannot deduct some rather important expenses connected with earning their salaries, such as the cost of getting to work and the expense of suitable clothes.

The tax rates for corporations are also different. (Unincorporated firms are subject to the tax rates of the owners.) Corporations pay income taxes on a sliding scale; the great majority of profitable companies (those with income over $100,000) are in the top bracket, with a tax rate of slightly under 50 percent. A company must also pay income tax in each state where it has facilities.

OTHER BUSINESS TAXES

Most states and some cities impose a sales tax. Although this is a tax on the business, it is passed on immediately and directly to consumers, so that for practical purposes the business acts as a tax collector for the state.

Many cities require a company to have a license to conduct business. The fee for this license is often based on sales or on the number of employees or the value of assets located in the city. A company must also pay local property taxes on the value of any real estate it owns. Then, too, some states have a tax on the value of a firm's equipment, inventories, or both.

Because the total bill for all of these state and local taxes can be quite substantial, those cities and states with lower tax rates are acquiring more business and industry than those with higher tax rates. And many localities now offer special tax incentives to encourage businesses to relocate there.

METHODS OF INVENTORY VALUATION

A quick look at a few balance sheets will convince you that inventory is an important asset to most businesses. However, the values shown are subject to some debate. In fact, for every firm there is a *range* of possible dollar amounts that could be considered the value of the firm's inventory. Moreover, the higher the economic inflation rate, the wider that range is. Let's explore this point with a simple case study.

Suppose we own a men's clothing store. Among the items we carry are neckties, which cost us $13.50 each. About every other month, we receive a dozen ties and add them to our display. Near the middle of the year, the manufacturer notifies us of a price increase: the ties will now cost us $15. We adjust our selling price accordingly and continue to buy and sell the ties.

At year-end, our accountant suggests we take a physical count of the inventory, and among the items we tally are 20 of these ties. What is their inventory value? Well, if they were all ties for which we had paid $13.50, the value would be $270 (20 × $13.50). But if they were the ones that cost us $15, the total value would be $300. And if they were a mixture, the total value would be some intermediate amount. If we knew which ties cost what, we could figure the exact value, but they all look alike and we just can't be sure of each one's exact cost. So that we can be consistent year after year, we decide to select one of the three commonly used methods of inventory valuation.

The FIFO Method

One method is called *FIFO*, which stands for *first in, first out*. FIFO is based on the assumption that the inventory items are sold in the same order in which we purchased or made them; that is, when a customer bought a tie, he or she took the one that had been in the store the longest.

If we chose to use FIFO to value our store's inventory, we would assume that all of the $13.50 ties had been sold and that the 20 we have left at the time of inventory all cost $15 each. The value of inventory of 20 ties would be $300.

The LIFO Method

The second method is called *LIFO—last in, first out*. The assumption under LIFO is that customers always buy the item we purchased or made most recently. In that case, all of the $15 ties have been sold, and the 20 we have left are $13.50 ties with a total value of $270.

Of course, the LIFO assumption sounds a little silly. How can we sell the last item in first when we don't even receive it until the last? But you must remember that with LIFO and FIFO, we aren't actually considering the physical movement of items but the accounting movement of dollars.

The Weighted Average Method

The third of the popular methods of inventory valuation is a compromise—the *weighted average* method. If during the year we had purchased four dozen ties at $13.50 and two dozen at $15, the weighted average cost would be the total dollars spent on the ties divided by the total number purchased.

$$(48 \times \$13.50) + (24 \times \$15) = \$1,008$$

$$\$1,008 \div 72 = \$14$$

The inventory valuation of our 20 ties under the weighted average method would be $280 (20 × $14).

The Tax Effects of Inventory Valuation Methods

The tax effects of these methods relate to the way cost of sales (also known as cost of goods sold) is calculated. We'll illustrate using the two extrmes, FIFO and LIFO:

Neckties	FIFO	LIFO
Beginning of the year inventory	$ 216	$ 216
Add: Purchases	1,008	1,008
Goods available for sale	1,224	1,224
Less: End of the year inventory	300	270
Cost of sales	$ 924	$ 954

The cost of sales, of course, is a tax-deductible expense. By switching from a FIFO to a LIFO basis, we increase that expense by $30. The resulting profit is decreased by $30, and the income tax paid is correspondingly less. If our store were in a 50 percent tax bracket, our taxes under LIFO would be $15 ($30 × .50) less because of the imported ties. When you consider that the same effect occurs with all the other items we carry in inventory, the tax saving can come to a respectable amount.

In some large corporations, the amount of the "LIFO reserve"—the difference in inventory value and cost of sales between FIFO and LIFO—is in the hundreds of millions of dollars. In 1979, three corporations—

AMOCO, General Electric, and U.S. Steel—together saved more than $3 billion in taxes by using LIFO accounting.

In addition to altering the company's tax bill, the choice of an inventory valuation method affects the company's financial statements. Here's how.

In an inflationary period, LIFO tends to understate the current value of the inventory on the balance sheet. However, it also results in a more realistic income statement, as the cost of sales more closely approximates what the merchandise would cost today. This higher cost of sales results in both lower profits and lower taxes.

The tax savings under LIFO is, in theory, only a tax deferment until a later date; that date comes, however, only when inventory is reduced, which rarely happens in a growing company. However, in a depressed economy, some companies do reduce inventory. As a result, their sales are, in part, matched against older, less expensive inventory. This results in a somewhat misleading increase in income and taxes, such as Texaco experienced in 1981.

FIFO, of course, has the opposite effect of LIFO on the financial statements. Here the inventory valuation on the balance sheet is more realistic. Profits on the income statement, however, are inflated because the cost of sales is lower than it would be in today's market.

At this point you're probably wondering why any company uses FIFO, since the tax benefits of LIFO are so substantial. In an inflationary economy, the trend is definitely to LIFO. However, for a company that is losing money or is only marginally profitable, LIFO's tax savings are of little value. In fact, a few years ago, the Chrysler Corporation switched to FIFO in an effort to preserve some profit. More importantly, many shareholders prefer FIFO because it does result in higher earnings as well as increased assets on the balance sheet. And, of course, if the price of the items in inventory decreases (as have the prices of pocket calculators and microcomputers), the tax advantage is with FIFO.

So, as you can see, circumstances determine which method of inventory valuation is best for a particular firm. For those companies seeking a middle ground between the two extremes, there is always the weighted average method. (There's one other method, said to be used by unsuccessful firms: FISH—"first in, still here.")

FIXED ASSET VALUES AND DEPRECIATION METHODS

As we noted in Chapter 3, the term *fixed assets* refers to a company's land, equipment, buildings, and vehicles—technically, any asset that has a useful life of more than one year. All these assets, except for land, are depreciated over several years; that is, their balance sheet values are lessened each year in accordance with one of the approved methods of *depreciation.*

This annual writedown is accomplished by creating a depreciation expense, an expense that is tax deductible, like any other. Unlike other expenses, however, depreciation expense does not involve a cash payment to anyone; it is merely a bookkeeping entry. So while depreciation lowers profits, it actually saves a company cash to the extent that it reduces income taxes.

Over the years, the federal government has sought to encourage business to buy more capital equipment (a fancier term for fixed assets) by permitting accelerated depreciation—a faster writeoff of assets. This technique allows companies to take tax deductions today that otherwise would be taken some years in the future. It is, in effect, a postponement of some of their taxes for a few years. While the postponement eventually ends as the equipment gets older, new postponements arise as long as the firm keeps buying more assets. The postponements created usually exceed the ones coming due, so that the total pool of taxes deferred by the use of accelerated depreciation tends to increase gradually year by year.

Government regulations affecting depreciation change fairly often. In the Economic Recovery Tax Act of 1981 (ERTA), Congress made major alterations to depreciation practices. These changes simplified a company's choices of depreciation methods and reduced the time periods during which items may be depreciated. Our discussion will focus on post-ERTA practices, not on methods in use prior to that time. Note, too, that while the information in this chapter was current at publication time, some further legislative changes may have occurred since then.

One change Congress made was to replace the word "depreciation" with the pharase "accelerated cost recovery"—quite a mouthful. The new term indicates that assets will no longer be depreciated over their useful lives. Instead, the assets' costs will be "recovered" over a much shorter period. Not only does this enable a company to convert its assets to expenses more quickly, but it also eliminates the frequent and bitter arguments between the company and the IRS as to what the useful lives of assets should be.

The ACRS Method

Under the *accelerated cost recovery system (ACRS)*, a fixed asset is written off over 3, 5, 10, or 15 years. The 3-year category includes automobiles, light trucks, machinery and equipment used in connection with research and experimentation, and any other assets which the IRS previously allowed to be depreciated in 4 years or less. The 5-year category includes petroleum storage tanks, single-purpose agricultural and horticultural structures (the government's name for henhouses), and everything that doesn't fall into the 3-, 10-, or 15-year categories. The 10-year category is for railroad tank cars, theme park structures (your local roller coaster), and certain types of public utility equipment, while 15 years is for buildings and other public utility equipment.

Once an item is classified, the company uses the appropriate depreciation table to determine what percentage of the item's cost should be expensed that year. These depreciation tables are prepared by the federal government and modified periodically. For example, for a 5-year asset acquired in 1982, 15 percent of its cost would be written off the first year, 22 percent the second, and 21 percent a year for the remaining 3 years.

The Straight-Line Method

Besides the ACRS system, the only alternative depreciation method now available to companies is straight-line depreciation. Under the straight-line method, the amount of depreciation for a particular asset is the same each year. The annual charge is simply the cost of the asset (under current law, salvage value is no longer deducted) divided by the number of years. Thus, if an asset cost $100,000 and was depreciated by the straight-line method over 5 years, the annual depreciation expense would be $20,000 ($100,000 ÷ 5).

With straight-line depreciation, the company selects the number of years in which the asset is to be depreciated, using the following guidelines:

- If the asset has a 3-year value under ACRS the company may choose 3, 5, or 12 years for straight-line depreciation.
- If the asset has a 5-year ACRS value, the straight-line choices are 5, 12, or 25 years.
- If the asset has a 10-year ACRS value, the straight-line choices are 10, 25, or 35 years.
- If the asset has a 15-year ACRS value, the straight-line choices are 15, 35, or 45 years.

A profitable, growing company will normally choose ACRS as its depreciation method. But if a company's profits are minimal or nonexistent, it may elect to depreciate an asset by the straight-line method over a longer period, thus reserving some of the depreciation expense to offset future revenues.

DEPRECIATION ON FINANCIAL STATEMENTS

While a company must use the same method of inventory valuation on its financial statements and its tax returns, the same does not hold true for depreciation. While most companies elect to use an accelerated depreciation method (ACRS being the current one) for tax purposes, they use straight-line depreciation on their financial statements. They do that because that straight-line spreads out the depreciation evenly, whereas accelerated methods create peaks and valleys. Thus, with straight-line, shareholders don't have to determine how much of a drop in income is due to accelerated depreciation rather than to other causes.

However, if a company uses straight-line depreciation on its financial statements, it must use the following recovery periods:

- 5 years for all items in the ACRS 3-year category
- 12 years for all items in the ACRS 5-year category
- 25 years for all items in the ACRS 10-year category
- 35 years for all items in the ACRS 15-year category

DEFERRED TAXES

Accelerated depreciation generates greater depreciation expense and lower taxes than straight-line in the early years, but there is a catch-up in the later years. At the end of the last year, the total deductible expense is the same no matter which method is used. Thus, the depreciation on a $100,000 asset written off over a five-year period would total $100,000 regardless of the method used.

The advantage of the accelerated method lies in putting off the payment of the taxes for a while and being able to use that money—like an interest-free loan—in the business. Moreover, in an inflationary economy, the dollars treated as an expense today are worth considerably more than the same number of dollars a few years later.

The amount of taxes that are postponed is shown in the "liabilities" section of the balance sheet as *deferred income taxes*. Deferred income tax is a rather peculiar liability. In theory, the deferred taxes will eventually have to be paid. But, in practice, this debt is almost *never* paid, because the company is continually adding to its tax deferment by buying more equipment. The total pool of deferred income taxes will come due only if the firm quits buying new equipment. That usually happens only when a company goes out of business, and then there is often too little money left to pay taxes anyway.

Because for many firms deferred income tax is a debt that is never paid, some analysts are inclined to overlook it when estimating a company's financial strength. In fact, the FASB is now deliberating the issue of whether or not deferred income tax should still be considered a liability.

INVESTMENT TAX CREDITS

The government gives companies yet another incentive for buying fixed assets: the *investment tax credit (ITC)*. A tax credit is a direct reduction in a business's or individual's taxes. For example, if you install storm windows on your house, you may reduce your tax bill by a certain percentage of the cost of the windows.

An investment tax credit provides the same benefit to businesses when they acquire depreciable assets (with the exception of buildings). If the asset is in the 3-year ACRS category, the company receives a 6 percent tax credit. If the asset is in the 5-, 10-, or 15-year categories, the credit is 10 percent. For a $100,000 asset depreciable over 5 years, the company would receive a $10,000 tax credit in the year in which the asset was placed in service. While the maximum amount of tax credits used in one year may not exceed the company's total tax liability for the year, the firm may carry the credit back 3 years, then forward up to 15 years. Thus, the credit could be used to reduce a prior or future year's taxes.

If a firm takes the tax credit, it must reduce the asset's depreciable value by one-half the tax credit. Thus, we could depreciate only $95,000 of our $100,000 asset ($100,000 − $10,000/2). Or, if the firm prefers, it may take a lower tax credit (4 percent for 3-year assets, 8 percent for all others) and depreciate the full cost of the asset.

As with depreciation, new legislation relating to tax credits is frequently enacted. In addition, IRS rulings in this area are rather complex. The finance department, as a result, continually faces the unenviable task of keeping abreast of corporate tax-related legislation and rulings.

Chapter 8

Analyzing
Financial
Statements

Contrary to most people's expectations, financial statement analysis is more an art than a science. While it makes use of mathematics and statistics, it's not simply "number crunching." The mathematical tools produce data, not explanations; information, not interpretation; measurement, not meaning. To these tools you must add judgment, which develops slowly—mostly out of experience. Every time you analyze a financial statement, you'll get better at making such judgments.

At times, the challenging part of financial analysis is not knowing what to look for, but finding the information on the statements. Although financial statements have been around for hundreds of years, their formats are standardized only in a general way. Where every doctor would use the same term to describe a particular part of the anatomy, different companies may use different terms for the same items on their financial statements. However, with a little practice, you'll find yourself reading most financial statements quickly and easily.

To help with our explanation of statement analysis, we have reproduced part of the 1981 annual report of the Gannett Company. Gannett calls itself an "information company." In plain English, the firm owns several dozen radio and television stations and newspapers. We'll analyze Gannett's balance sheet and income statement; as you learned in Chapter 3, these are the two most important financial statements.

ANALYZING THE BALANCE SHEET

The balance sheet is especially useful in analyzing a company's financial condition. In fact, some firms call their balance sheet their "statement of financial position" or "statement of financial condition."

While the balance sheet states the financial and physical resources a firm has for carrying on business in the future, it makes no judgment about how well those resources will be used. Since every business transaction changes the balance sheet, keep in mind how current the balance sheet is when you are doing a financial analysis.

Now let's examine the major balance sheet accounts, examples of which are presented in Figure 8-1. Most balance sheets include notes which are too long and complex to appear here. You can see that in Figure 8-1 some lines refer to individual notes.

Current Asset Accounts

Current assets are all those assets the firm expects to convert to cash within one year after the balance sheet's date. The major current asset accounts are normally Cash, Accounts Receivable, Inventory, and Prepaid Expenses.

Cash

Whenever a company has more cash than it can use within the next few days, the firm is likely to invest this money in marketable securities such as treasury bills, certificates of deposit, and commercial paper. (See Chapter 15 for more information on cash management.) These investments may be listed below Cash either as "short-term investments" or "marketable securities" (the latter being Gannett's choice of terms). More often, though, the amount is simply added to Cash and the invested amount shown in parentheses with a brief explanation. As long as these investments are secure and can be easily sold, they are considered to be cash equivalents.

Figure 8-1.   Balance sheet for Gannett Co., Inc.

Consolidated Balance Sheets
Gannett Co., Inc. and Subsidiaries

Assets

	December 27, 1981	December 28, 1980
Current Assets:		
Cash	$ 24,423,000	$ 9,971,000
Marketable securities, at cost, which approximates market	64,055,000	17,105,000
Trade receivables (less allowance for doubtful receivables of $5,382,000 and $5,253,000 respectively)	172,590,000	147,331,000
Other receivables	10,425,000	11,046,000
Inventories (Note 4)	34,058,000	25,978,000
Prepaid expenses	18,830,000	15,025,000
Total Current Assets	324,381,000	226,456,000
Property, Plant and Equipment:		
Cost (Note 5)	818,413,000	712,607,000
Less accumulated depreciation	(273,938,000)	(233,175,000)
Net Property, Plant and Equipment	544,475,000	479,432,000
Intangible and Other Assets:		
Excess of acquisition cost over the value of assets acquired (less amortization of $49,197,000 and $38,315,000 respectively)	514,410,000	476,699,000
Other assets	64,842,000	29,153,000
Total Intangible and Other Assets	579,252,000	505,852,000
Total Assets	$1,448,108,000	$1,211,740,000

Liabilities and Shareholders' Equity

	December 27, 1981	December 28, 1980
Current Liabilities:		
Current maturities of long-term debt (Note 6)	$ 65,147,000	$ 10,601,000
Accounts payable:		
Trade	80,648,000	43,066,000
Other	9,472,000	9,762,000
Accrued liabilities:		
Compensation	32,801,000	23,675,000
Taxes—other than income	3,381,000	3,246,000
Pension, profit sharing and other (Note 7)	24,524,000	26,206,000
Dividend payable	22,867,000	20,135,000
Income taxes (Note 8)	46,712,000	66,168,000
Deferred income	10,245,000	8,343,000
Total Current Liabilities	295,797,000	211,202,000
Deferred Income Taxes (Note 8)	68,465,000	49,593,000
Deferred Compensation and Other Liabilities	26,002,000	17,102,000
Long-Term Debt, Less Current Portion (Note 6)	221,469,000	167,860,000
Shareholders' Equity: (Note 9)		
Preferred stock, par value $1.00: Authorized 2,000,000 shares; Issued—None		
Common stock, par value $1.00: (Note 9) Authorized 100,000,000 shares; Issued—53,044,694 shares and 52,882,513 shares respectively	53,045,000	52,883,000
Additional paid-in capital	93,389,000	91,630,000
Retained earnings	689,941,000	621,470,000
Total Shareholders' Equity	836,375,000	765,983,000
Commitments and Contingent Liabilities (Note 10)		
Total Liabilities and Shareholders' Equity	$1,448,108,000	$1,211,740,000

Consequently, we treat them as cash for the purpose of statement analysis.

Accounts Receivable

Accounts receivable, or trade receivables, are the money customers owe the firm. This account may also include some small amounts due from employees, affiliated companies, or other noncustomers. The figure shown in less an allowance for bad debts or doubtful receivables.

When a company separates its trade receivables from other receivables, as Gannett does, we leave out the "other receivables" in some financial ratio calculations. This is because amounts included in Other Receivables—for example, a debt owed to the firm by an affiliate—are often less certain to be paid than the trade accounts. Trade credit, however, is generally reliable, and since most companies sell their products or services on credit, this is usually one of their more important assets.

Inventory

Inventory may be shown as one figure, or, in the case of a typical manufacturer, it may be broken down into raw materials, work in process, and finished goods. Inventory is a primary asset for many firms. It has been referred to as the "graveyard of American business," because too much or undesirable inventory is frequently given as the major cause of a business's failure. In its Note 4, indicated after "Inventories," Gannett explains that its inventories consist mostly of newspaper printing supplies.

Prepaid Expenses

The Prepaid Expenses account comprises rent, insurance, interest, and other costs paid in advance. These items don't exactly fit the definition of current assets because they aren't turned into cash. However, they are used up in a year, as well as being a comparatively small amount for most companies. Hence, we, like most analysts, will treat them as a current asset.

Noncurrent Asset Accounts

Noncurrent assets consist of fixed assets, long-term investments and receivables, intangibles, and any other miscellaneous assets. In general, these assets are used—and often used up—in running the business, instead of being converted to cash as current assets are. However, they can be sold, so there is potential cash value here even though its realization is not expected.

Fixed Assets

Fixed assets are properties, plants, equipment, and vehicles—the materials that it takes to manufacture products and run a business. Gannett gives just one total figure for all its fixed assets, but breaks this number into a half-dozen categories in the footnotes to the financial statements.

As we discussed in Chapter 3, fixed assets (except land) are listed at their historical cost less depreciation accumulated to date. Hence, the numbers don't show the effects of inflation on current values. In many cases, the amounts given are nowhere near the cost of replacing those assets or the current market price if they were to be sold. While this practice sounds like a serious problem for the analyst, it really isn't. The equipment and buildings will eventually become worthless through time and use, and price variations in the interim are not normally of much consequence. As for land, while it often increases in value, unless the company plans to sell it, the increased value is not of great concern in a short-term financial analysis. If, on the other hand, you were planning to buy the company, you would consider the current values of fixed assets very closely.

Long-Term Investments and Receivables

Some balance sheets show long-term investments and receivables and even special cash funds as noncurrent assets. This is not because these assets are any less liquid or any less secure than those in the Current Assets section, but because the company does not expect to convert them to cash or use them up in the coming year.

Intangible Assets

Intangible assets are found on perhaps one out of three financial statements. Such assets include patents, copyrights, and licenses. However, the one we are usually concerned with is goodwill, which occurs when one company buys the assets of another and pays more for them than their book value.

A few down-to-earth companies simply label this item ''goodwill'' on the balance sheet, but most prefer some more lengthy phrasing. Most of the time, the phrase will include the word *excess*. For example, Gannett uses the phrase "excess of acquisition cost over the value of assets acquired."

Goodwill is amortized, or written off, over a period of time (up to 40 years). Therefore, on the balance sheet, the Goodwill account is shown with all accumulated amortization subtracted.

Other Assets

Most balance sheets contain a catch-all account called Other, Miscellaneous, or Sundry Assets. These may sound suspicious because they don't fit any of our standard categories; but unless they represent 10 percent or more of the total assets, you can usually accept them at face value.

Current Liabilities

Current liabilities are debts that are due within one year. The list usually includes accounts payable and accrued liabilities, and perhaps some notes and loans payable, taxes, customer deposits, and so on. The pressure a company feels to pay its current liabilities is similar to the pressure that we as individuals feel to pay our own bills. Most of us, however, have a steady salary that enables us to plan our payments well in advance. The revenues of a business are dependent on the sales volume and speed of collections and, hence, are much less certain.

Notes and Loans Payable

Notes and loans payable are often listed first, although from a legal standpoint they have no priority over any of the other debts. To the analyst, a bank loan is usually a sign that the company is established and stable enough to satisfy the fussiest of creditors. But banks intend to be paid, and their loan terms usually have little leeway when it comes to repayments.

Accounts Payable

The accounts payable—mostly to suppliers—are nearly always a major item, but they do have a fair amount of elasticity. If the average terms call for payment in 30 days, most firms can stretch them to 60 days or even 90. This stretching is sometimes done with the supplier's consent, but more often without it. The analyst would like to know how far the payables are already stretched, but the normal financial statement does not give enough information to tell that. Consequently, outsider analysts are obliged to buy reports from credit agencies to see how promptly suppliers are being paid.

Accrued Liabilities

Accrued liabilities (or expenses) are a permanent fixture like accounts payable and usually fluctuate within a moderate range. These required payments for wages, vacation pay, and various taxes can seldom be put off without difficulty.

A Word About Advance Payments

One type of current liability that does not appear on Gannett's balance sheet—advance payments from customers—is different from the others in that the company will pay in goods or services rather than in money. With accrual accounting we do not consider such advance payment as a revenue until the company earns it by providing the goods or services. Magazine publishers often have this type of entry because they receive subscription payments in advance. Each month, as the magazines are delivered, an appropriate portion of this liability is converted to revenue. In fact, another name for advance payments is deferred revenue.

Long-Term Debts

Long-term debts are those due more than a year from the date of the financial statement. Any portion of a long-term liability due within the coming year is classified as current—as is the first item Gannett lists under Current Liabilities.

These obligations are eyed less severely by the analyst simply because they lack the urgency of short-term debts. Of course, these debts will have to be paid someday. But companies that are able to obtain long-term financing in the first place—and you have to be pretty well established to qualify—can most often refinance those debts later on.

While individual debts are retired as planned, new ones arise to take their place, and the total pool of long-term debt seldom diminishes. A company's ability to perpetuate long-term debt is tied to its outlook for profits. Should the outlook be for losses, the firm's problems will be compounded by the difficulty of refinancing its long-term liabilities.

Liabilities for future pensions and other types of deferred compensation are also easily managed so long as a company operates successfully. They do, however, become one more problem should the situation change for the worse.

As we discussed in Chapter 7, deferred income taxes arise from a company's use of accelerated depreciation for tax purposes. In the great majority of cases, the taxes coming due are more than offset by the deferrals arising from newly purchased assets. Thus, the total pool of deferred taxes seldom goes down until a company stops buying new equipment, which is usually at the end of its existence. (Note the rise in Gannett's deferred income taxes between 1980 and 1981.)

As long as a company keeps growing and the government continues its current depreciation policy, this theoretical debt never gets paid. As a result, analysts debate whether or not deferred income tax is a liability. To be conservative, you would count it as one.

The long-term liabilities may include *convertible bonds or notes* (although not in Gannett's case). Analysts favor these obligations because if all goes well, they will be converted to common stock instead of being repaid—a double financial benefit to the firm. The debt won't be converted if things don't go well, which is, ironically, when the firm would benefit most from such conversion.

Minority Interest

Found on perhaps one out of five financial statements, *minority interest* is often placed either among long-term liabilities or between them and the equity accounts. A Minority Interest account appears when a company consolidates in its financial statements the statements of a subsidiary of which it owns less than 100 percent. All the subsidiary's assets and liabilities are added to the parent company's accounts, but only the portion of the subsidiary's equity that the parent owns can be added to its own equity. The part it doesn't own is the minority interest.

Consequently, minority interest doesn't fit into our regular categories. It's not a liability, because it has to be repaid only if the subsidiary is liquidated; yet it's not equity, because it belongs to someone outside the shareholder family of the parent corporation. We suggest that in analyzing financial statements that include minority interest, you take the minority interest off the liability side of the balance sheet and deduct an equal amount from the total assets before doing your analysis.

Equity

The equity accounts represent the permanent capital, or net worth, of a business. All the assets purchased with equity money are dedicated first to the payment of the firm's liabilities; so the greater the equity, the better the chance a company has to attract lenders.

The Equity section of a financial statement may include several accounts, but it's the total of these accounts that concerns the analyst. Consequently, it is seldom necessary to distinguish among them for analysis unless you are considering investing in the company.

The Equity section has two main parts. One details the money invested by the shareholders; on Gannett's balance sheet, it is the sum of the equity accounts titled Preferred Stock, Common Stock, and Additional Paid-in Capital. The other represents money from profits that have been kept or reinvested in the business—the Retained Earnings account.

Two other equity accounts, though they appear infrequently, get special attention from analysts. One is redeemable preferred stock, a stock issue that the company intends to buy back and may even have a set schedule for doing so. Such preferred stock looks more like a liability than equity. However, while it is outstanding, it is legally subordinate to the debts of the business.

The other account is *treasury stock,* common stock the firm has bought back. This account has a debit balance and is thus a negative amount in equity. When a company buys back its own stock, it is returning money to the investors. This may weaken the support for creditors. In large amounts, treasury stock may also be a sign that a firm has reached its limits of expansion and can find nothing better to do with the cash it generates than return it to the shareholders. More positively, the existence of treasury stock may mean the firm plans to offer the stock to employees through an ESOP (Employee Stock Ownership Plan) or to use it to purchase another company.

ANALYZING THE INCOME STATEMENT

The income statement reveals a firm's performance in a given time period—usually one year. It's a statement of the sales made, minus the expenses incurred, and the resulting profit or loss.

Income statements say nothing about the firm's present financial condition, but they do offer some hints about the future. The trend of sales and expenses over the recent past—say, five years—can be expected to continue roughly in the same direction, assuming no major changes in circumstances. Profits, however, are not so easily forecast. They are a small part of total sales (5 or 6 percent for the typical company), so even minor changes in sales volume or total expenses can dramatically affect net income.

Revenues

Sales are the principal revenues of most companies. When other revenues, such as interest or royalty income, contribute more than 10 percent of the total, it is a matter of interest to the company, but not necessarily of concern.

Sometimes a portion of income is labeled "extraordinary" or "nonrecurring." You can see an example of this in Gannett's income statement (Figure 8-2) just above Net Income. In this case, the extraordinary income was a gain on the sale of a television station. These revenue distinctions can be useful to an analyst who is trying to forecast future revenues.

Figure 8-2.   Income statement for Gannett Co., Inc.

Consolidated Statements of Income

Gannett Co., Inc. and Subsidiaries

	Fiscal Year Ended		
	December 27, 1981	December 28, 1980	December 30, 1979
Net Operating Revenues:			
Newspaper advertising	$ 787,282,000	$ 710,512,000	$ 638,428,000
Newspaper circulation	260,637,000	227,293,000	194,013,000
Broadcasting	141,392,000	122,079,000	106,212,000
Outdoor advertising	155,647,000	135,106,000	110,450,000
Other	22,213,000	19,993,000	16,141,000
	1,367,171,000	1,214,983,000	1,065,244,000
Operating Expenses:			
Cost of sales and operating expenses, exclusive of depreciation	727,116,000	656,169,000	570,181,000
Selling, general, and administrative expenses, exclusive of depreciation	227,039,000	199,938,000	175,398,000
Depreciation	46,966,000	40,487,000	35,231,000
Amortization of intangible assets	11,186,000	10,190,000	8,181,000
	1,012,307,000	906,784,000	788,991,000
Operating Income	354,864,000	308,199,000	276,253,000
Non-Operating Income (Expense):			
Interest expense	(25,757,000)	(22,042,000)	(22,094,000)
Interest income	3,028,000	3,788,000	8,915,000
Other	5,771,000	11,290,000	6,007,000
	(16,958,000)	(6,964,000)	(7,172,000)
Income Before Income Taxes and Extraordinary Items	337,906,000	301,235,000	269,081,000
Federal and state income taxes (Note 8)	165,400,000	149,250,000	135,000,000
Income Before Extraordinary Items	172,506,000	151,985,000	134,081,000
Extraordinary items, less income taxes of $7,800,000 (Note 3)			9,200,000
Net Income	$ 172,506,000	$ 151,985,000	$ 143,281,000
Income Per Share:			
Income before extraordinary items	$3.17	$2.81	$2.50
Extraordinary items (Note 3)			.17
Net Income	$3.17	$2.81	$2.67

Operating Expenses

The principal item under Operating Expenses is cost of sales, also called cost of goods sold (discussed in Chapter 3). This refers to the cost of making or acquiring the products that are sold. The cost of sales is usually more money than all the other costs put together, and it should move up and down in proportion with the sales figure. If it doesn't, there will probably be a wide variation in profits from one year to the next. Note that Gannett's income statement does not give a separate cost of sales figure, but includes other operating expenses except for depreciation. Such an approach makes it more difficult to compare this company with others.

Operating expenses are meant to be the "normal" costs of carrying on the business and exclude such "nonoperating" costs as interest expense. We might argue that interest costs have become pretty normal themselves in modern business, but it's a matter of little importance. The operating income, income before taxes, and income before extraordinary items all fade into insignificance as we approach the bottom line.

The bottom line, net income (also called net profit), is pretty much the last word on what a company accomplished the previous year. The annual report may contain a dozen pages praising or explaining the past year's activities, but when the smoke is blown away, it is the net income figure that yields the final appraisal.

Publicly held corporations go a step beyond the net income figure by dividing it by the number of common shares outstanding to obtain an earnings per share (EPS) figure. EPS is significant to investors who occasionally see net income go up but EPS come down because more shares have been issued during the period.

FINANCIAL STRENGTHS AND WEAKNESSES

The financial health of a business consists of three major characteristics: liquidity, leverage, and profitability. These refer to internal conditions of the company that are largely within the control of management. Of course, a firm's condition may also be affected by factors, such as the state of the economy, that are beyond management's control.

Liquidity

Liquidity refers to the ability of a company to generate enough cash to pay its bills and expenses on time. In the operating cycle of most businesses, cash is invested to acquire inventory, inventory is sold to produce accounts receivable, receivables are collected to generate cash, and the process is repeated all over again—or, rather, it is continuous.

Most businesses rely to some extent on credit to finance part of this process and have a series of debts gradually moving toward their due dates. The problem of liquidity management is simply to generate enough cash in the normal cycle to pay the debts as they mature. We can expect, for example, that a liability due in 90 days will be paid by the sale and subsequent collection of some products now sitting in inventory.

The liquidity problem is complicated, however, because the cash inflow is uncertain while the required outflow is inflexible. Creditors expect their money when promised, just as employees expect regular paychecks. However, the cash being generated does not follow a set schedule. Sales of inventory vary, as do collections from customers. Because of this difference between cash generation and cash payments, businesses must maintain a certain ratio of current assets to current liabilities in order to ensure adequate liquidity.

Leverage

Leverage refers to the relationship between a firm's total liabilities and equity—the mix between the money creditors contribute to a business and the amount investors put in. A company is said to be highly leveraged when it has a lot of debt in relation to equity.

Entrepreneurs like leverage because they believe that they can earn enough on the borrowed funds both to pay the interest and to make a good return for themselves. From that perspective, the more leverage you have, the better; leverage will increase profits.

But leverage can increase losses, too; when times are tough, those interest payments can be a real burden—sometimes an overwhelming one. So creditors—banks in particular—keep a wary eye on a debtor's leverage. When it starts to get too high, they shy away from extending more credit to that company.

It's hard to say at what point a company begins to have too much leverage, for each creditor has its own opinion on the matter. A little further on, however, we'll give some guidelines that work pretty well.

Profitability

If running a business is like baking a pie, then profit or loss is the crust that makes it either a gourmet's delight or a distasteful flop. And you can never be entirely sure about which it's going to be. The profitability of a firm depends on many factors, some of which can be controlled, others not.

Demand for the product or service is the key element, perhaps more important than all the others put together. Demand will either be there or not. It's something that has to arise in the customers themselves, although effective marketing can do a great deal to awaken it. The fundamental question in business is, "If we make this product, will enough people buy it to give us a profit?" And while market research gives some indication of the answer, the acid test occurs when the company actually tries to sell the item.

Management, according to one recent survey, contributes about 20 percent to the success or failure of a business. Good managers come in all sizes and shapes, but the one characteristic common to them all is an eagerness to succeed.

A depth of resources—financial, physical, and human—enables a company to sail through the daily ups and downs and occasional crises of commercial activity. The first sign that a business may not be a going concern will start a desertion among customers, creditors, employees, and investors that will only hasten its demise.

Our last major profit factor tends to get ignored. Yet, except for demand, it is as important as any other profit factor. It's *luck.* No matter how well managed or otherwise equipped for success the firm is, if it starts making recreational vehicles just before an oil crisis hits the country or building houses just as interest rates head for a new peak, it's got troubles.

There are, of course, many other factors that affect profits. We could mention location for retail businesses, sources of supply for oil businesses, and so on. But whatever the factors needed for success, the right combination will be reflected in that bottom line, and that's where we look to judge success.

MEASURING A COMPANY'S FINANCIAL CAPABILITY,

Measuring the liquidity, leverage, and profitability of a company is not a matter of how many dollars in assets, liabilities, and equity it has, but of the *proportions* in which such items occur in relation to one another. We analyze a company, therefore, by looking at ratios rather than just dollar amounts. More than 150 financial ratios are currently in use. Each analyst has his or her particular favorites, and there is a continuing debate about which are the most useful.

Several years ago co-author James E. Kristy developed a system of analysis using five basic ratios. These ratios provide a measure of about 80 percent of a firm's financial strength. Other ratios can then be used to complete the picture.

The Kristy method works well for analyzing most kinds of businesses: manufacturers, retailers, service companies, large and small companies, and public and private firms. However, two industries should not be measured with this set of ratios: financial firms (such as banks, insurance companies, and investment companies) and government-regulated firms (such as utilities). You'll need specialized knowledge to analyze companies in these two industries because they differ in important ways from most other companies.

The five ratios are used for making a short-term analysis, which is the most common type. Such an analysis assesses the company's current financial strength. Different ratios are utilized for the purpose of measuring a firm's long-term prospects or for analyzing its value as an investment.

A critical requirement in ratio analysis is a standard of excellence for each ratio. The standards used here were developed by Kristy and form the basis of a point scoring system called the Commerical Credit Matrix™. With this system, all five ratios are used in judging a company; use of fewer ratios can give a distorted view.*

An alternative to using uniform standards is to compare the firm's key ratios with average ratios for other companies in the same industry. With some specialized ratios such as inventory ratios, industry averages are particularly important. One excellent source of industry averages is *Annual Statement Studies,* published each September by Robert Morris Associates (P.O. Box 8500, S-1140, Philadelphia, PA 19178). Dun & Bradstreet and many industry associations also publish averages for financial ratios.

The Ratios

The first three ratios measure liquidity. This characteristic is emphasized because in a short-term analysis it is the most critical element. If a company has a problem with its leverage or profit—the factors measured by the other two ratios—it generally has some time (maybe six months or even a year or two) to solve it. But if the firm runs out of cash for even a short time, it can be in real trouble.

---

*For a complete description of the system, see *Analyzing Financial Statements: Quick and Clean,* 4th ed. (1983), by James E. Kristy; available from Books on Business, Box 313-D, Buena Park, CA 90621.

Current Ratio (CR)

$$\frac{Current\ assets}{Current\ liabilities} = current\ ratio$$

Standard of excellence: 2.00 to 1

The *current ratio* is the granddaddy of financial ratios and relates the two key elements of liquidity. The use of 2 as a standard of excellence is also well established. By such a standard, we mean that a current ratio of 2.00 to 1 or somewhat higher is considered excellent. For all of the ratios presented here except return on equity, the standards of excellence represent optimum ratios. Ratios better than the standards aren't necessarily harmful, but they don't add much to a company's overall effectiveness.

In the case of Gannett, the current ratios are 1.09 and 1.07 for 1981 and 1980, respectively. (Throughout the discussion on ratios, all Gannett's statistics are shown and calculated in rounded millions. For this ratio and the next three, the statistics are taken from Figure 8-1.)

For 12/27/81	For 12/28/80
$\frac{324}{296} = 1.09$	$\frac{226}{211} = 1.07$

Both are below the standard; in fact, we consider them to be ''poor'' current ratios. They may result from the fact that, like most other communications firms, Gannett does not have a large inventory. (Inventory, of course, is a major component of current assets.) However, that lack of inventory also means that Gannett hasn't the large reserve of products ready to be sold that the typical manufacturer has, and it should manage its current liabilities with that fact in mind.

Remember, though, that we've looked at only one of the liquidity ratios. This system is designed so that weakness in one area can be compensated by strength in others.

Quick Ratio (QR)

$$\frac{Cash + accounts\ receivable}{Current\ liabilities} = quick\ ratio$$

Standard of excellence: 1.00 to 1

The *quick ratio,* sometimes called the "acid test ratio," is also well known among analysts, and its standard of excellence is widely accepted. This ratio focuses on the "quick," or most liquid, current assets—cash and receivables—and thus provides a closer look at the firm's debt-paying ability than the current ratio does.

In this ratio and the next one, the cash amount should include any short-term investments (sometimes called marketable securities) listed in the Current Assets section of the balance sheet. Also, the accounts receivable figure includes only those amounts due from customers: the trade receivables.

Thus, Gannett's QRs are:

For 12/27/81

$$\frac{24 + 64 + 173}{296} = \frac{261}{296} = .88$$

For 12/28/80

$$\frac{10 + 17 + 147}{211} = \frac{174}{211} = .82$$

These are slightly less than the standard of excellence. We call them both "good," and they partly compensate for the company's low current ratios.

Liquidity Ratio (LR)

$$\frac{Cash}{Current\ liabilities} = liquidity\ ratio$$

Standard of excellence: .40 to 1

The *liquidity ratio* (also called the cash ratio and the super-quick ratio) eliminates all current assets except the one actually used to pay current liabilities: cash, including cash equivalents.

For the Gannett Company, the LRs are as follows:

For 12/27/81

$$\frac{24 + 64}{296} = \frac{88}{296} = .30$$

For 12/28/80

$$\frac{10 + 17}{211} = \frac{27}{211} = .13$$

Gannett's 1980 LR was "poor," but it improved to "good" in 1981. If the company's three ratios are taken together, in 1980 the poor-good-poor array would average out to a "fair" liquidity position. The 1981 combination of poor-good-good is a definite improvement; hence, we might say that Gannett has a "good minus" or "pretty good" liquidity position. Most of the improvement is centered in the Cash account, although the quick ratio has also improved.

Equity/Debt Ratio (ED)

$$\frac{Equity}{Liabilities} = equity/debt \ ratio$$

Standard of excellence: 1.75 to 1

The *equity/debt ratio* is a measure of a company's leverage. It compares the number of dollars invested by shareholders to the amount being contributed by creditors. The higher the ratio, the lower the leverage, and the more comfortable or flexible the firm's debt obligations are.

Before calculating leverage, most analysts adjust the equity figure by subtracting all intangible assets. The rationale for this adjustment is that if the company were to be liquidated, it's unlikely that intangible assets such as goodwill could be converted to cash. The real value of these assets comes from the future profits they are expected to generate. Because such estimates are difficult to make, many analysts are reluctant to accept asset values based on them. However, analysts' opinions on this point vary.

Normally, intangible assets are a small amount and subtracting them has little effect on the ratios. But Gannett's goodwill is over a half billion dollars, and its treatment will significantly affect the analysis.

For 1981, Gannett's tangible equity is $322 million ($836 million − $514 million); in 1980, it is $289 million ($766 million − $477 million). Gannett's EDs then are:

For 12/27/81	For 12/28/80
$\dfrac{322}{296+68+26+221}=\dfrac{322}{611}=.53$	$\dfrac{289}{211+50+17+168}=\dfrac{289}{446}=.65$

Because we made a large deduction of intangibles from equity, the ratios for both years are low compared to the standard. According to this ratio, then, Gannett's leverage was high.

High leverage, or heavy indebtedness, affects corporations the same way it does individuals: there is a greater risk that the borrowers will be unable to pay their debts. Consequently, additional credit, if needed, is harder to get. Moreover, most commercial loans have a variable interest rate—one tied to the banks' prime rate, the one charged the most creditworthy customers. When interest rates are high, therefore, a company with heavy leverage is at a disadvantage in competing for credit against a company with low leverage. If it passes along its higher interest costs to its customers, the firm may lose business to the competitor with less debt.

Return on Equity (ROE)

$$\frac{Net\ income}{Equity} = return\ on\ equity$$

Standard of excellence: .14 to 1

Return on equity is the most fundamental of the ratios; it belongs to the family of return on investment (ROI) ratios which, as we will discuss further in Chapter 9, answers the question, "Do we have a business here?" This ratio is one measure of a firm's profitability, telling us what return the company has earned on the shareholders' investment. As we mentioned earlier, the higher the return, the better, from the investor's point of view. While our standard of excellence is .14, this standard fluctuates somewhat with interest rates and the rate of inflation. When rates are higher, a company must have a higher ROE to satisfy its investors.

While one poor showing on ROE seldom means failure, a string of them points toward that conclusion. A company with a poor ROE outlook has difficulty attracting additional investment to cure its problems or to expand.

Having deducted intangibles to calculate equity/debt, we use the same tangible equity to compute the ROE ratio. Net income is found on Figure 8-2. For Gannett in 1981 the ROE is .54; for 1980 it is .53:

For 12/27/81

$$\frac{173}{322} = .54$$

For 12/28/80

$$\frac{152}{289} = .53$$

Both figures are extraordinary; seldom does a business have a ratio half that high. The results, of course, are greatly affected by the deduction of intangibles. The same process that hurt the company's equity/debt ratio has boosted its ROE.

Also, we must bear in mind that heavily leveraged companies tend to have higher ROE's than less leveraged firms. That's because a heavily leveraged company generates its income from a relatively small amount of investors' capital and a large amount of borrowed capital. Hence, the percentage return on investors' capital is higher than for a comparable firm that is less leveraged.

Summing Up

The five ratios we have presented constitute only a small number of the tools financial analysts work with. But they account for a large proportion of the results analysts are able to achieve. The financial strength of a firm is centered in its liquidity, leverage, and profitability. Remember that a weakness in any one area can be offset (for a while, at least) by strength in the other two, and all five ratios are needed to form a well-rounded opinion.

We might sum up our analysis of the Gannett Company by saying that in 1980 the firm had fair liquidity, a poor leverage position, and excellent profits; overall, a fair (as between poor and good) financial position. In 1981, that position became "fairly good" because of an improvement in liquidity.

This is the result of a traditional analysis, where the value of intangible assets is not counted. Because of the large amount of goodwill on Gannett's balance sheet, this represents a significant adjustment and a challenge to the analyst. Let's look at what the ratios would be without making that adjustment.

First, the three liquidity ratios are not affected. Second, the unadjusted equity/debt ratios are as follows:

For 12/27/81

$$\frac{836}{296+68+26+221} = \frac{836}{611} = 1.37$$

For 12/28/80

$$\frac{766}{211+50+17+168} = \frac{766}{446} = 1.72$$

While neither year's ratio quite meets the standard of excellence, both are considerably improved.

Third, to recalculate the ROEs:

For 12/27/81   For 12/28/80

$$\frac{173}{836} = .21 \qquad\qquad \frac{152}{766} = .20$$

These ratios are still excellent in both years. Thus, when the intangible assets are not eliminated, Gannett's financial position can be considered fairly good in 1980 and quite good in 1981.

Chapter 9

Measuring ROI,
or
Do We Have
a Business?

In French, ROI means king. In Business, ROI means *return on investment,* and it is king. That's because ROI addresses that fundamental question, "Do we have a business here, or are we wasting time and money?" In free-enterprise societies, ROI is the lure that attracts capital to new business ventures. When ROI is high, investment money flows like a swollen river; when it is low, zero, or negative, the river runs dry.

ROI RATIOS

ROI is a ratio, arrived at by dividing investment into return. There are several different meanings for both "return" and "investment." In fact, ROI is a term that has come to be applied to a whole family of ratios, some of which are more useful than others. In this chapter, we'll discuss the ones you're most likely to encounter.

Return on Equity (ROE)

The most fundamental of all ROI ratios is the one you've already encountered: *return on equity (ROE)*. You'll recall from Chapter 8 that the formula for ROE is:

$$\frac{Net\ income}{Equity} = return\ on\ equity$$

In this case, the return is net income—profit after taxes and everything else, the bottom bottom line. Investment in this case is equity, a corporation's net worth. ROE is critical because it's the figure that will attract and hold the capital necessary for the business to operate. Investors watch ROE closely, for as a general rule, they want to invest in the firm that will bring them the best return.

The ROE we've just described is the *corporate* return on equity. But what about the individual who purchases stock after the company was started and wants to measure his or her *individual* return? The answer is—you guessed it—another ratio: *shareholders' return on equity*. This ratio is calculated as follows:

$$\frac{Earnings\ per\ share}{Market\ price\ per\ share} = shareholders'\ return\ on\ equity$$

Note that the earnings figure the shareholder uses is not the profit for the past year, but the expected profits in the future. Depending on whether the earnings seem to be growing or shrinking, the new stockholder will pay more or less for the stock than the company's ROE would indicate.

As we mentioned in Chapter 8, one current standard for an excellent company ROE is .14 (14 percent) or better. Many companies consistently (for a time, anyway) earn returns over 14 percent. Those that do may find competitors trying to share their good fortune.

Sometimes, the high earners are protected from competitors by having an exclusive patent, a valuable location, or other special feature. For many years, General Motors had ROEs of over 20 percent. GM was effectively shielded from new competition by the enormous cost of the plants, materials, and people needed to enter the auto business—until foreign competitors backed by their own governments accumulated sufficient wherewithal to penetrate the U.S. market with competitive products.

If a firm's ROE drops too low and appears to be staying down there, management may seek out new products, new markets, or even an entirely new business to rejuvenate the ratio. The current scramble by large, mature corporations to merge with or acquire others is motivated chiefly by the desire to bolster a sagging ROE or one that is expected to sag. If these firms had excellent prospects of their own, they would reinvest their extra cash in their own expansion instead of using it to buy other companies.

If ROE drops to the approximate level of after-tax interest on a savings account and if the prospects for new products are dim, the firm may be approaching its last days. The business student would tell the corner grocery to become a supermarket, the copper mining company to promote penny collecting as a hobby, and the railroads to sprout wings. But such things are easier said than done, and sometimes the answer to the question asked by ROI (in the chapter title) is, "No, not any longer."

Return on Sales (ROS)

Another popular ROI ratio is *return on sales (ROS),* also called the *profit margin:*

$$\frac{Net\ income\ (or,\ sometimes,\ pretax\ income)}{Net\ sales} = return\ on\ sales$$

For example, if a firm earns $1 million on sales of $20 million, its ROS or profit margin is .05, or 5 percent. Or you could say that the firm makes 5 cents profit on every dollar of sales.

Most companies that issue annual reports calculate ROS, but it is not as useful as its popularity might indicate. The average overall ROS for nonfinancial American companies is about 5 percent, plus or minus 1 or 2 percent (depending on the economy). But there are some big differences in the averages for the industries making up that overall average. The *pretax* ROS for manufacturers of cosmetics averages about 7 percent, while the same figure for grocery stores is about 2 percent. The ROS pattern for any particular industry depends on the demand for its type of product, the intensity of competition, and the amount of capital assets needed for that kind of business.

Thus, it's impossible to give a general standard of excellence for this ratio, and that is the main reason the ratio is not very helpful to managers. Moreover, ROS doesn't always reflect what's happening to the final arbiter, ROE. The average pretax ROE for cosmetics manufacturers is 22 percent; the average for grocery stores is 28 percent.

To some extent, a company may choose the ROS it would like to have. That is, there is often a tradeoff between the volume of sales and the return on sales. Some stores, such as K Mart, strive for high sales volume by offering discount prices. For these firms, we'd expect a low ROS as a result. In contrast, stores like Saks Fifth Avenue have a lower volume of sales but most likely a higher return on the sales they do have. To decide which store is really doing better, we would check their ROEs.

Return on Assets (ROA)

Another prominent ROI indicator, particularly among large corporations, is *return on assets (ROA)*:

$$\frac{Pretax\ profit,\ (or,\ sometimes,\ net\ income)}{Total\ assets} = return\ on\ assets$$

Several variations of this ratio make adjustments to that "total assets" denominator.

ROA reveals what kind of profit the company has made in relationship to all its resources—its assets, which you remember are the sum of its liabilities and equity. ROE, however, shows the relationship of profit to the shareholders' portion of the business, leaving out liabilities because creditors do not share in profits; their rewards are interest payments, the cost of which has been deducted in arriving at the profit figure.

Return on assets, which leaves in the liabilities, is usually of less interest to shareholders than is return on equity. ROA's greatest use is in measuring the performance of departments, divisions, and sometimes subsidiaries of large corporations.

A division does not have a balance sheet separate from that of the corporation because, for legal and financial purposes, it is part of an undivided whole. Therefore, we cannot allocate a corporation's equity or liabilities to its various divisions and calcuate their ROEs.

No matter. ROA is a good internal management ratio because it measures profit against all of the assets a division uses to make those earnings. Hence, it is a way to evaluate the division's profitability and effectiveness. It's also more appropriate here because division managers seldom get involved in raising money or in deciding the mix between debt and equity. Instead, when they need money, they request it from corporate headquarters.

There is a similar reason for using pretax profit in the ROA calculation. Tax strategy is managed at the corporate core. A division manager is often not aware of—much less in control of—the earnings or losses of other divisions. It may be that the profit from one division will be entirely offset by the losses of another, so that there will be no taxes to pay at all. In such a case, after-tax earnings of the profitable division are meaningless.

One of the cardinal rules in managing business professionals is to hold them accountable only for those activities they control. ROA comes close to measuring just that. When it doesn't, the ratio can be adjusted to fit the situation. As a result, you may encounter some special types of ROI ratios.

Special Forms of ROI

In dealing with ROI ratios other than the three we've just discussed—ROE, ROS, and ROA—it's a good idea to have the user define the ratio. That's because users calculate ratios differently. Also, there are many different ROI ratios, with new ones being thought up all the time. Here a few of the most common special forms, along with their usual meanings.

Return on Net Assets (RONA)

When you see the word *net* in business, it implies that something has been subtracted from something else. Frequently, the items deducted from total assets to arrive at net assets are the funds attributed to "free," or no-interest, credit—primarily accounts payable to suppliers. There may be other types of deductions in addition to, or instead of, this one, so you should have the user define this ratio.

Return on Net Capital Employed (RONCE)

"Capital employed" can mean either equity or liabilities plus equity; usually the money from free credit sources is netted out. One large firm calculating RONCE starts with total assets and then deducts the following "interest-free" debt:

- Accounts payable
- Accrued liabilities
- Income taxes payable
- Other current liabilities
- Deferred income taxes
- Minority interests

If RONCE sounds suspiciously like RONA, that's no accident. They're often the same—but not always.

Return on Gross Assets (ROGA)

Our final ROI ratio sounds like one of those old sci-fi movie monsters, but it really stands for *return on gross assets*. ROGA is much like RONA with some or all of the deducted assets put back. "Gross" usually means before any deductions. Companies using ROGA as a measure often include a proportion of the company assets that are shared by all divisions, such as the corporate headquarters.

SETTING A PROFIT GOAL

Setting a profit goal for a business is a little like setting a happiness goal for yourself. People and corporations seem to have an endless capacity for more. So the primary profit goal of a business, though it may not be so stated, is to get as much profit as it can.

Here, however, we're talking about setting a goal for the financial plan. This goal gives managers a mark to strive for, defines the performance that will keep the stockholders happy, and determines the profit figure above which management can pay itself a bonus.

A good place to start is with some fairly common standard of excellence, such as the ROE measure in the Commercial Credit Matrix discussed in Chapter 8: 14 percent after taxes. Next, examine the past ROEs for the company. If the firm has consistently been earning 16 to 18 percent, you don't want to pick a lower figure for your profit goal. Unless there is new information, you can assume that the conditions that allowed the company to earn so high a return in the past probably still prevail.

Finally, look at the conditions that have changed:

1. The state of the economy: Is it heading up or down?
2. Your products: Has anything new and exciting been added?
3. Your competitors: Are there more or fewer of them?
4. Your prices: Can you raise them to cover added costs?

Depending on how you answer, these factors should cause you to add or subtract a point or two from your goal. Profit goals should be realistic— that is, achievable. But it doesn't hurt any to pick a figure that everyone has to stand on tiptoes to reach.

BREAKEVEN ANALYSIS

Breakeven is the point at which sales (or revenues) equal expenses. The technique of breakeven analysis is something nearly every business student encounters because it focuses on the razor's edge that separates profit from loss. Breakeven analysis also takes a bit of calculation and gives a specific answer, which makes it a good exam question.

But is it useful in the real world of business? Often, but not always. Breakeven analysis requires a fine distinction between fixed and variable costs, a precise separation to which real expenses seldom submit. Hence, somewhat arbitrary distinctions must be made. Also, in real life, management cannot control all factors affecting the business, and those uncontrollable elements can sabotage a well-planned analysis.

However, regardless of one's feelings about the practicality of breakeven analysis, the concept behind it is not merely important to the understanding of business: it is almost essential. The idea that increased volume can bring greater profits is understood by almost everyone, but ignorance of exactly how this principle works has been a key element in many business failures.

The assumption behind breakeven analysis is that every sale entails two kinds of expenses: variable and fixed. *Variable costs* are those that rise and fall as sales do, and that you wouldn't have at all if you didn't make any sales. Some obvious examples are direct labor and materials and salespersons' commissions.

Fixed costs are expenses that remain constant over the short term, regardless of sales volume. Rent on the property, depreciation on the equipment, and administrative salaries are examples. Assuming that a company's products are sold for more than the variable costs, the excess can go toward paying the fixed costs, and the dollar amount of sales that exactly pays off the fixed costs is the breakeven point. It is the volume of business the company must achieve before it can begin making a profit.

Let's say, for example, that we are a book publisher and we produce a book that sells for $10. We have the following variable costs:

Royalties	$1.50
Reseller's discount	4.00
Printing cost	2.50
	$8.00

Our fixed costs include the editor's and typesetter's time and a share of the office overhead, a total of $10,000. How many books would we have

Figure 9-1. Breakeven chart.

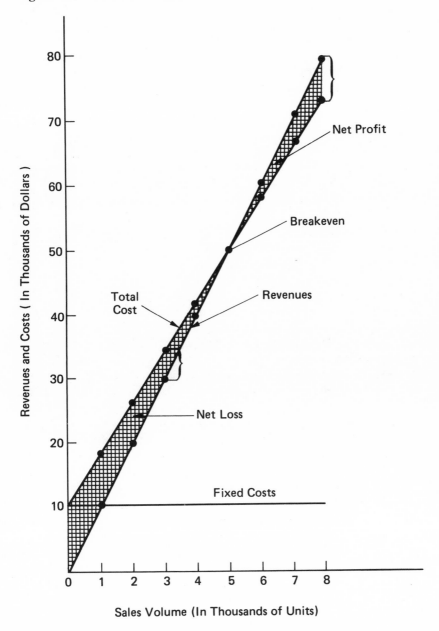

to sell to break even? The answer is 5,000 copies, since we have $2 per book to cover the $10,000 in fixed costs ($2 × 5,000 = $10,000). Once 5,000 books are sold and the fixed costs are paid, every extra $2 becomes pretax profit. For that reason, the difference ($2) between the price per unit ($10) and the variable cost per unit ($8) is called *marginal income*.

The breakeven point can also be drawn on a graph (see Figure 9-1) or expressed as an equation. If:

$$VC = variable\ costs$$
$$FC = fixed\ costs$$
$$S = dollars\ of\ sales$$
$$P = profit$$

Then,

$$P = S - (VC + FC)$$

Since at breakeven our profit is 0, the equation then becomes:

$$0 = S - (VC + FC),\ \text{or}\ S = VC + FC$$

Next we substitute the appropriate percentage of *S* for *VC*. Using our example above, variable costs are $8 of the $10 sales price, so $VC = .8S$. What's more, we know that the fixed costs are $10,000, and we can also substitute that value in our formula:

$$S = .8S + \$10,000$$

Then we solve for *S:*

$$S - .8S = \$10,000$$
$$.2S = \$10,000$$
$$S = \$50,000$$

To have sales of $50,000, we'd have to sell 5,000 books at $10 apiece.

Chapter 10

Measuring Cash Flow

Cash flow is one of those financial terms that has several meanings. Sometimes when businesspeople speak of cash flow, they simply mean the amount of money that comes in the mail each day or that amount minus the checks that are written. But the most common definition of cash flow, the one used by financial people, can be expressed as an equation:

$$Cash\ flow = net\ income + depreciation$$

or, to be a little more precise:

$$Cash\ flow = net\ income + noncash\ expenses$$

You'll recall from earlier chapters that depreciation is a noncash expense. So, too, is *amortization,* a systematic writeoff process, similar to depreciation, that is applied to intangible assets like goodwill and to leasehold improvements. (We'll discuss amortization in regard to leasing in Chapter 21.)

Depreciation and amortization expenses are subtracted from revenues to arrive at profit, but no cash is paid out to anyone to defray those expenses. They are merely accounting entries. By adding them back to profit, we obtain the amount of extra cash—the cash flow—generated by the business during the year or other accounting period.

Although the extra cash is being generated every day, cash flow can only be calculated whenever a business first figures its net income. The great amount of cash coming in and going out every day makes it difficult to judge the extent of the cash flow, or even whether it is positive or negative. Think of the times you thought your own cash position was good until you discovered a repair bill that had fallen behind the dresser.

Companies experience the same problem. They don't drop invoices behind the dresser, but they may have hundreds of employees incurring financial obligations. Consequently, it is not uncommon to misjudge the amount that will have to be paid out in even the next 30 days.

Managing cash flow is especially difficult for a fast-growing company. The growth of sales means a growth in assets, and, Santa Claus aside, assets arise only from the laying out of cash. Thus, companies that are growing rapidly—say, by 20 percent or more per year—often have to scramble for the cash needed to finance their expansion. It is a paradox of business that firms with little or no profits and little or no growth usually have fewer cash problems than high profit, rapid-growth companies.

Co-author James E. Kristy has termed this financial paradox "the noncash illusion," referring to his idea that the cash flow equation as stated above is incomplete and should be restated as follows:

Cash flow = net income + depreciation − added assets

Cash flow is generally thought of as discretionary or extra money. But in the day-to-day business of replacing worn-out assets and handling increasing orders, much of this "discretionary" cash gets spent even before management is aware of how much there is—or, rather, was.

Other financial experts recognize the limitations of the traditional cash flow model. Writing in the August 1981 issue of the *Harvard Business Review,* researchers Bradley Gale and Ben Branch drew a distinction between *gross* cash flow (profit + depreciation) and *net* cash flow from a formula similar to Kristy's. Warning executives that control of cash "is a slippery and complex problem," their article demonstrates how the rapid growth of a business drains cash.

Of course, companies can finance part of their growth with borrowed money, and most do so. But in the act of relieving a cash pinch by borrowing, a firm may be compounding an already troublesome leverage condition. As we discussed in Chapter 8, a company's liquidity, leverage, and profitability are interrelated. Each must be managed with an eye to the total effect.

"A CRUEL" ACCOUNTING: HOW IT COMPLICATES CASH FLOW MANAGEMENT

Some of the difficulties of cash flow management can be attributed to the accrual method of accounting. Because of a desire for accurate income statements, accountants have wrenched revenues and expenses away from their natural companion, cash. Like two rivers split at their origin, profit flow and cash flow meander their separate ways.

As a result, it is not total sales that reflect the cash coming into a business each year. Instead, it is total sales minus or plus the increase or decrease in accounts receivable during the same period. A company just starting out, giving generous credit terms, and growing fast may collect only half of its sales in the first year. The reverse applies to expenses and accounts payable. The lag between making a purchase (when it officially counts as an expense) and paying for it must be considered in cash planning.

Accrual accounting sets other traps for the cash manager, such as customer payments in advance for orders. Those appear as a liability on the balance sheet: "Customer deposits." But it is a liability that will be paid with goods, not cash. Another example is income tax. This is a significant and urgent expense, but much of it may end up as deferred tax and, as we saw in Chapter 7, may never be paid.

WORKING CAPITAL

Out of the struggle to measure and control cash flow has come the concept of *working capital*. This is another one of those terms that has acquired varied meanings. By the term some people mean simply cash; others think of it as cash and available credit. But the most common definition—and among finance people the one used nearly exclusively—is:

Working capital = current assets − current liabilities

In a sense, the current assets and current liabilities represent the active parts of a business: the activity related to making and marketing the products or services and collecting the money due. This activity is endless. Although the accounts involved are continually churning, it is clear upon inspection that they represent as permanent a fixture as the land and buildings and the shareholders' equity.

As long as a company sells on credit, it will have accounts receivable; if the sales are growing steadily, you can count on the receivables to do the same. Ditto for inventory. Like other assets, these are purchased—directly in the case of inventory, indirectly in the case of receivables—with cash. And they represent a permanent investment.

The need for cash to finance them, however, is mitigated somewhat by the equally permanent current liabilities. As a company grows, it makes more products, hires more people and, if all goes according to plan, pays more income taxes. These increases will cause increases in accounts payable, accrued expenses, and accrued income tax. Such increases, as long as they are maintained, can be said to finance part of the current assets. By subtracting the one from the other, we obtain working capital—the part of current assets that is financed with equity money or long-term loans.

From this explanation, you might come to think that the less working capital a company has, the better. After all, if the company can finance most or all of its current assets with other people's money, it will need less of its own. This is not the case, however, because another important rule in managing current assets and current liabilities is that you maintain more of the former in order to be sure of promptly paying the latter.

Recall our discussion in Chapter 8 about the importance of having a good liquidity position. One measure of that was the current ratio, which comprises the same elements as working capital in ratio form:

$$\frac{Current\ assets}{Current\ liabilities} = current\ ratio$$

We suggested that a good current ratio is 2 to 1 because the requirement to pay current liabilities is specific and certain, while the conversion into cash of accounts receivable and inventories is somewhat unpredictable. And when we say that the current liabilities represent "permanent" financing, we really mean revolving financing—financing that can be renewed as long as the debts are paid when due and good relations maintained with the creditors.

So while it is pleasant for a company to have its suppliers, employees, and government finance some of its current assets, there can be too much of a good thing; it is necessary to strike a reasonable balance. You'll hear business professionals talk about "inadequate working capital" or, occasionally, "too much working capital," by which they mean this disharmony between current assets and current liabilities.

As popular as the term is, there are two serious problems with the concept of working capital. One is its expression as a dollar amount. If a firm has current assets of $3 million and current liabilities of $2 million, its working capital is $1 million. This figure sounds very much like cash. In fact, some people come to think of it as cash, or at least as "funds" that can be spent for this or that.

But working capital is neither. It is strictly a concept, not something that can be held in the hand or put in the pocket. You can deduct current liabilities from current assets all day long—on paper. But you can't do it in real life. Working capital does not pay liabilities. Only cash does that.

Nor does working capital represent discretionary funds or money. We've already seen how most current assets are like permanent investments. Perhaps some extra cash is available; perhaps the inventories can be reduced and the receivables shrunk; but the cash that will be rendered from that process cannot be foretold by working capital.

The second problem with working capital is even more critical than the first. It seems impossible to determine how much working capital is enough—or, for that matter, how much is too much or too little. As often as financial people talk about working capital, they have been unable to develop such a standard, which would make the concept of working capital truly useful in managing a business.

We do have such a theory about the current ratio. It says that the uncertainty of cash receipts vis-à-vis the certainty of cash payments may be offset for the typical business by a 2:1 ratio of current assets to current liabilities. And given the current assets and current liabilities that make a 2:1 ratio, we can, of course, calculate the working capital that is adequate for that specific situation.

But the dollar figure we come up with will apply only to that case and may not suffice in another. The following comparison illustrates the problem of interpreting working capital:

	Company A	Company B
Current assets	$500,000	$200,000
Current liabilities	400,000	100,000
Working capital	100,000	100,000
Current ratio	1.20	2.00

Both companies have $100,000 of working capital, yet their current ratios clearly indicate that Company A has a much weaker liquidity position.

The term *working capital* is a convenience when you are talking about starting new projects or ending old ones. Each business venture requires some investment in current assets; each provides some of the financing in the form of current liabilities; the net amount—working capital—is the money the company has to supply. But even though the concept is useful in financial planning, the management of working capital is a difficult task. It is hard enough just to manage cash. When you throw in much larger accounts like receivables, payables, and inventory—all of which affect one another, all of which are in a state of flux, and all of which you have little information about until some time after the fact—the complexity of the job sometimes makes it seem unmanageable.

THE STATEMENT OF CHANGES

We didn't find many nice things to say about the statement of changes in financial position in Chapter 3, and we haven't altered our opinion. But we should, at least, give the accounting profession credit for good intentions. The idea behind the statement of changes is to reveal how the balance sheet has changed during the year or other period. That may be important information if we are trying to find out where our cash has gone. Many businesses generate a good cash flow during the year only to find that the extra money was completely absorbed by inventory or receivables. So good management includes an analysis of which activities generated cash and which used it up.

The statement of changes does this, all right, but in a way that is so complicated and intricate that it discourages general use. Here we will give a short description of the statement of changes and then suggest some simpler ways of obtaining the same information.

Figure 10-1 presents statements of changes of the Gannett Company for three years. Note that the figures represent *changes during the year* and not the values of accounts at some particular time. Thus the statement of changes shows activity during a period, not the status of various accounts on a certain date.

The statement of changes is divided into two main sections—Sources of Working Capital and Uses of Working Capital. For the moment, think of working capital as cash. The Sources section details the actions and activities that brought cash into the company: net income (with depreciation and amortization added back), the issuance of more stock, the sale of certain fixed assets, additional long-term loans, and so on.

Figure 10-1.　Statement of changes for Gannett Co., Inc.

**Consolidated Statements of Changes
in Financial Position**

Gannett Co., Inc. and Subsidiaries

	Fiscal Year Ended		
	December 27, 1981	December 28, 1980	December 30, 1979
Sources of Working Capital:			
Income before extraordinary items	$172,506,000	$151,985,000	$134,081,000
Add (deduct) income charges (credits) not affecting working capital:			
Depreciation	46,966,000	40,487,000	35,231,000
Amortization of intangibles	11,186,000	10,190,000	8,181,000
Gain on sale of certain assets	(995,000)	(7,862,000)	(4,149,000)
Deferred income taxes	18,872,000	9,265,000	5,596,000
Other	3,113,000	4,766,000	4,448,000
Working capital provided by operations	251,648,000	208,831,000	183,388,000
Working capital provided by (used for) extraordinary items:			
Proceeds from the sale of television station WHEC including gains and deferred income taxes of $7,800,000			25,241,000
Costs of early extinguishment of debt, net of current taxes			(1,700,000)
Common stock issued	4,433,000	10,060,000	9,743,000
Retirement of debt from exercise of warrants and conversion of convertible debt		(3,850,000)	(6,250,000)
Proceeds from sale of certain assets, net of working capital adjustments	4,548,000	18,715,000	13,499,000
Collections on long-term receivables	2,336,000	2,858,000	2,578,000
Increase in long-term debt	59,134,000	165,135,000	21,608,000
Total	322,099,000	401,749,000	248,107,000
Uses of Working Capital:			
Dividends declared	83,235,000	72,870,000	60,234,000
Additions to property, plant, and equipment	102,478,000	83,093,000	68,933,000
Payment and current maturities of long-term debt	6,961,000	120,816,000	168,604,000
Acquisition of subsidiaries, net of working capital adjustments:			
Net tangible assets, principally property, plant, and equipment	12,161,000	24,890,000	29,093,000
Excess of acquisition cost over the value of assets acquired	48,593,000	92,970,000	37,978,000
Debt assumed on acquisitions	(1,709,000)	(3,871,000)	(8,511,000)
Repurchase of warrants, net	23,312,000		
Investment in tax leases, net	25,698,000		
Other	8,040,000	5,207,000	3,486,000
Total	308,769,000	395,975,000	359,817,000
Increase (Decrease) in Working Capital	$ 13,330,000	$ 5,774,000	($111,710,000)

The Uses section shows how the money was spent. Some went for dividends, some to pay off long-term loans, some to acquire other companies, and so on. You can see from the way items are presented that the approach is highly technical. It almost seems as if, partway through this statement, the accountants forgot what it was they had set out to do—that is, show the changes in balance sheet accounts.

Even after wading through this accounting morass, you still don't have all of the balance sheet changes. This just gives you the changes in the noncurrent accounts; that is why the statement speaks of sources and uses of working capital rather than of cash. To find the changes in such accounts as Receivables, Inventories, and Short-Term Loans, you must refer to Changes in Components of Working Capital. Do you begin to suspect that the accountants aren't trying to make it easy for you?

If you are unfamiliar with accounting terms and principles and you still want to know the changes in certain balance sheet accounts from one year-end to the other, the direct approach works much better. Many companies list two or more balance sheets side by side so the reader can make comparisons. One obvious way of seeing how much things have changed is to subtract the earlier figure from the later for the accounts you are interested in.

Let's say, for example, that you wanted to know if the Gannett Company's net fixed assets went up or down in the year ended December 27, 1981. The 1981 annual report gives the following figures (the balance sheet for that year is reproduced in Chapter 8):

	12/27/81	12/28/80
Net Property, Plant and Equipment	$544 million	$479 million

The difference is easily found by subtracting: the company's net fixed assets increased $65 million in 1981.

In contrast, try to find that figure on the company's Consolidated Statements of Changes in Financial Position. To do so you would start with the additions to property, plant, and equipment; subtract depreciation; subtract proceeds from the sale of certain assets; add (or subtract the negative number) gain on the sale of certain assets; and add the acquisition of subsidiaries/net tangible assets. That would bring you within a couple of million dollars of the $65 million we arrived at above—about as close as it is possible to get with the statement of changes.

You may wonder if the American Institute of CPAs or the SEC or somebody isn't trying to improve the statement of changes. Well, yes. The Financial Accounting Standards Board is looking into it. However, the board is acting (as it should) with deliberation, so it may be a couple of years before we see anything better. Meanwhile, others have suggested various new formats. We'll discuss just one of those here.

THE DELTA FLOW STATEMENT

In 1977 co-author James E. Kristy developed a simplified format to use in place of the statement of changes and called it the Delta Flow Statement. It is pictured in Figure 10-2. This statement was designed as a supplement to the Commercial Credit Matrix (described in Chapter 8), to be used if there were unusual changes in the ratios or if the analyst

Figure 10-2. Delta flow statement.
    © **1977 James E. Kristy. Used with permission.**

DELTA FLOW STATEMENT

By_____ **J EK**

Company _____ GANNETT CO., INC. _____

Date _____ 1-12-83 _____

Instructions: Show changes in the balance sheet from one period to the next. Increases are shown as (+) amounts, decreases as (−) or in brackets ( ).

☐ Thousands
☒ Millions

		Date:	12-27-81			
		Period:	Year			

SOURCES OF CASH

1	Net Income	$ 173	$	$	
2	Less Dividends	(83)			
3	Other Capital Accounts Repurchase of warrants	(20)			
4	**NET WORTH**	70			
5	Long Term Debt	54			
6	Deferred Liabilities	28			
7	Minority Interest				
8	Other				
9	**DEFERRED OBLIGATIONS**	82			
10	**LONG TERM SOURCES** *Lines 4 plus 9*	152			
11	Accounts Payable	37			
12	Notes Payable	55			
13	Other	(7)			
14	**CURRENT LIABILITIES**	85			
15	**TOTAL SOURCES OF CASH** *Lines 10 plus 14*	237			

USES OF CASH

16	Net Fixed Assets	65			
17	Intangibles	38			
18	Other Slow Assets	36			
19	**NON-CURRENT ASSETS**	139			
20	Accounts Receivable	25			
21	Inventories	8			
22	Other	4			
23	**CURRENT ASSETS** except cash items	37			
24	**TOTAL USES OF CASH** *Lines 19 plus 23*	176			
25	Cash Increase (Decrease) *Lines 15 minus 24*	61			
26	Working Capital Increase *Lines 10 minus 19*	13			

The items listed as Sources or Uses of Cash normally increase as a company grows. If an item is a negative amount, that is, the balance sheet amount declined from one year to the next, instead of being a source of cash it will be a use, and vice versa.

wanted more details about the changes. The ratios give a quick and composite picture; the Delta Flow Statement (or the statement of changes) describes how the picture came to be.

Except for the first two lines, the Delta Flow Statement simply lists the differences in the accounts of successive balance sheets. It starts with the accounts in the Equity section, proceeding through Long-Term Debt and then Current Liabilities. The same format, slow to current, is followed for the assets in the section headed Uses of Cash. (A slow asset is one that, under normal circumstances, does not convert to cash within one year). The language is plain, and there are no odd twists. You'll notice our figure of $65 million for the changes in net fixed assets on line 16.*

The measurement of cash flow is of the greatest importance to companies that are growing rapidly. Businesses that have found their niche and are content with it, like the local shoe repair shop, can probably be run with little more financial information than the annual income tax return. But it's the ones in the fast lane that excite us. They are also the ones that need the most management expertise. We try to help you acquire a little more of that in the next chapter.

*The Delta Flow Statement and the booklet describing it, *Analyzing Financial Statements: Quick and Clean,* are available from Books on Business, Box 313-D, Buena Park, CA 90621.

Chapter 11

Replacement and Growth Analysis

Since businesses are guided by people, it should not surprise us very much that they have some human failings. One such failing seems to be an innate resistance to planning ahead. This resistance is due partly to the difficulty of predicting the future and partly to our reluctance to expend time and mental effort preparing for events that may never occur. In fact, some good arguments can be made against sacrificing a lot of time from doing business in order to plan it. But one part of planning that is essential to most firms is planning for the replacement of fixed assets.

On a personal level, we may put off thinking about buying a new dishwasher or vacuum cleaner until the one we have quits. The resulting annoyance is our own. But when the equipment of a business breaks down, it is often the customers who suffer, and customers have a low tolerance for inconvenience. So the replacement of fixed assets in business usually has an air of urgency about it unless it is carefully planned in advance.

Business has the mechanism of depreciation for approximating the gradual loss of the value of fixed assets. Each year, part of the cost of a depreciable asset is written off, or expensed. If a company were to set aside an equivalent amount of cash each year, it would automatically accumulate funds for replacing those assets. But few firms do this. The cash represented by depreciation is almost always used for the current needs of the business. The concept of cash flow, discussed in Chapter 10, lumps the depreciation money with profits and considers it all "discretionary" funds. Thus, there is a need to plan not only the replacement of worn-out equipment but also the financing of such replacements.

INFLATION ACCOUNTING

A serious complication to replacement planning has arisen in the last two decades: relatively high and persistent inflation. In the first half of this century, the average annual inflation rate was a negligible 2 percent. Since then, however, the U.S. economy has seen rates as high as 13 percent, and the current (1984) outlook is still for moderately high rates— perhaps averaging 7 percent over the next 10 years.

A simple example illustrates the problem that inflation poses. Let's say a company buys a forklift truck today for $18,000 with the expectation of using it for six years. If the forklift industry is subject to 7 percent annual inflation over that period, we can expect the cost of replacing that vehicle six years from now to be about $27,000.

Moreover, the company may want something a little more elaborate by then, perhaps a forklift equipped with a side-shifter or even one that is computer driven. As a result, the replacement unit might cost nearer $35,000.

Such conditions create *two* financial problems for the company: Besides having to come up with $27,000 or $35,000 at the end of six years, the company must decide how to account for the depreciation expense in the meantime. Under straight-line depreciation, the company would expense $3,000 per year to account for the machine's full historical cost of $18,000 by the end of its useful life of six years. But some people would argue that the writedown ought to be at least $4,500 per year because we expect it to cost the company $27,000 just to restore what it has now. To charge only $3,000 per year is to understate the "true" expense and to overstate the profits.

Despite these arguments, CPAs continue to depreciate historical rather than replacement cost, in accordance with generally accepted accounting principles. However, the Financial Accounting Standards Board (FASB) thinks enough of the other view to require that *large* publicly held corporations supplement their annual reports with information about replacement-cost depreciation. In this context *large* means having total assets of more than $1 billion or inventories and gross property, plant, and equipment of more than $125 million at the beginning of the year.

Figure 11-1 shows the price-level data in the Gannett Company's 1981 annual report. In the top half of the page are three versions of the income statement for the year. The first is the official one—the one using histor-

Figure 11-1. Income statement adjusted for changing prices for Gannett Co., Inc.

Consolidated Statement of Income
Adjusted for Changing Prices

(In Thousands)

Fiscal Year Ended
December 27, 1981

	Historical	Adjusted for general inflation (constant dollars)	Adjusted for changes in specific prices (current cost)
Revenues	$1,367,171	$1,367,171	$1,367,171
Expenses			
Cost of sales and operating expenses, exclusive of depreciation	727,116	729,813	729,488
Depreciation	46,966	76,197	63,244
Other operating expense	238,225	238,225	238,225
Non-operating expense	16,958	16,958	16,958
Provision for income taxes	165,400	165,400	165,400
	1,194,665	1,226,593	1,213,315
Net Income	$ 172,506	$ 140,578	$ 153,856
Gain from decline in purchasing power of net amounts owed		$ 22,511	$ 22,511
Effect of increase in specific price level on inventories and property, plant, and equipment held during the year			$ 69,090
Effect of increase in general price level			58,859
Excess of increase in specific price level over increase in the general price level			$ 10,231

At December 27, 1981, the current cost of inventory was $33,294; and the current cost of property, plant, and equipment, net of accumulated depreciation, was $781,836.

Five-Year Comparison of Selected Supplementary Financial Data
Adjusted for Effects of Changing Prices

(In Thousands Except for Per Share Amounts)	1981	1980	1979	1978	1977
Total Operating Revenues					
Historical	$1,367,171	$1,214,983	$1,065,244	$ 979,464	$ 785,511
Average 1981 dollars	$1,367,171	$1,341,010	$1,334,740	$1,365,435	$1,178,916
Historical Cost Information Adjusted for General Inflation*					
Income before extraordinary items	$ 140,578	$ 138,292	$ 143,754		
Income per share before extraordinary items	$ 2.59	$ 2.56	$ 2.68		
Net assets at year-end	$1,067,490	$1,057,645	$1,006,093		
Current Cost Information*					
Income before extraordinary items	$ 153,856	$ 153,050	$ 156,344		
Income per share before extraordinary items	$ 2.83	$ 2.83	$ 2.91		
Excess of increase in specific price level over increase in the general price level	$ 10,231	$ (9,145)	$ (20,460)		
Net assets at year-end	$1,072,972	$1,018,382	$ 983,041		
Gain from Decline in Purchasing Power of Net Amounts Owed*	$ 22,511	$ 26,845	$ 29,835		
Cash Dividends Declared Per Common Share					
Historical	$ 1.57	$ 1.38	$ 1.21	$ .93	$ .77
Average 1981 dollars	$ 1.57	$ 1.52	$ 1.51	$ 1.30	$ 1.16
Market Price Per Share at Year-end					
Historical	$ 34.00	$ 36.50	$ 31.92	$ 27.17	$ 25.25
Average 1981 dollars	$ 32.90	$ 38.48	$ 37.82	$ 36.48	$ 36.96
Average Consumer Price Index	272.4	246.8	217.4	195.4	181.5

*Amounts in average 1981 dollars.

ical costs. The second restates assets (and their depreciation expense) on a constant-dollar basis—that is, the original costs adjusted according to the changes in the Consumer Price Index (CPI). The third, using a current-cost approach, reflects changes in the prices of the kinds of equipment Gannett has; these costs have apparently increased less than the CPI.

The major change in the income statements is the depreciation expense. That change is then reflected in the net profit after adjusting it for the lower income tax that would have had to been paid on the reduced earnings.

The value to management and investors of this price change exercise is probably more apparent than real. The data suffer from the statistical procedure of changing one input while holding all the others steady. Very few events work that way in real life. In this case, for example, the price-adjusted income figures do not show the effect of inflation on the debts owed by the company. Debtors benefit from inflation because they repay loans with dollars that are worth less than those they borrowed.

In fact, the FASB has recognized that the usefulness of this data is questionable, and in June 1981 the board called for research on this issue. In a recent survey of controllers, only 13.7 percent strongly agreed that the data are effective, and the majority felt that annual reports with such data are not an improvement over annual reports without price-change adjustments. However, the vast majority of controllers did feel there was a need to provide financial data adjusted for changes in prices. So the dilemma remains, and the accounting profession must continue to grapple with it.

LIFE CYCLES

Companies, like governments and all other institutions made by people, are mortal. In the course of time, they are created, enjoy their season, and then vanish. The lifetime of a company ranges a scale perhaps twice the length of that for humans. A firm that has existed for 150 years has earned some distinction for longevity.

Products, too, have a limited existence. They survive as long as there is a demand for them. But that same demand that keeps them alive also attracts competitors. For every successful product, you can assume that a hundred companies or individuals are trying to come up with something better.

The theoretical life cycles of companies and products are similar except for the scale—shorter for products, longer for companies. As Figure 11-2 shows, the life cycle curve is a kind of lazy S starting at the bottom

Figure 11-2.   Theoretical life cycle of a typical company or product.

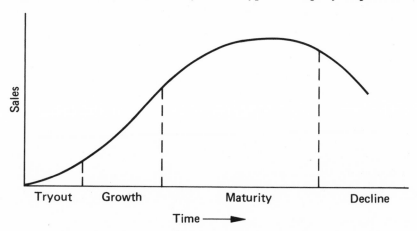

on the left, rising slowly through the tryout stage, picking up speed in the growth stage, leveling off as the company or product reaches maturity, and finally entering the downward curve of the S as it approaches the stage of decline.

The usefulness of life cycle theory is limited by its unrefined generalizations. Many companies and products do not follow the S pattern because of odd circumstances (we might as well call it luck—both good and bad) and, on rare occasions, a flowering of genius, which can appear without warning.

For example, the bicycle began to languish with the introduction of the mass-produced automobile in the 1920s. In 1960, only 3.7 million bicycles were sold in this country. But then an unpredictable interest in physical fitness breathed new life into the industry. In 1975, sales of bikes exceeded 14 million. Since then sales have ebbed and flowed like the tides under a full moon. As a result, a life cycle chart for the bicycle would look like waves on a rough sea.

Management invests considerable thought and effort in renewing the life of companies and products in the decline stage. Sometimes the simplest of changes will work. It has been said that offering a range of colors has sold more telephones for the Bell System than all its technological innovations put together. Declining after a splendid career, DuPont nylon was born again when someone came up with the idea of tinting hosiery.

The stages of the life cycle will determine management strategy. The time to experiment with a product is in the tryout stage. Once the growth stage begins, heavy promotion is needed. At maturity, much effort should be devoted to research and development so that the life cycle may be renewed. In the decline stage, it's time to salvage resources and turn to other products. (Would it have done the railroads any good, do you think, to advertise heavily when air travel began growing?)

MERGERS AND ACQUISITIONS

Companies in the early stages of the life cycle often have cash flow problems. Even though the firms are profitable, the financing of their growth often takes more funds than they generate. On the other hand, companies that have reached the maturity phase of the life cycle and are still profitable will typically generate more cash flow than they can use. Not that it is difficult to get rid of money, but sometimes it is difficult to invest the money so as to receive as high a return as the company is used to getting.

Companies have a multitude of investment opportunities just by virtue of being in business. The most obvious one is simply doing more of what they are doing—expanding their markets or their product line—assuming that the demand for their products at profitable prices is sufficient to support more of the same. Another investment opportunity is the creation of new products through research and development. When neither of these prospects is attractive because the company and its products are in the maturity stage, the firm will often seek to rejuvenate itself through a merger with or acquisition of another, more promising company.

Rejuvenation is not the only motive for merging, but it does lie behind a good many combinations of large, long-established corporations. The oil industry is a curious example. When the Arab oil crisis hit, several domestic oil companies issued public statements saying in effect that if they were allowed to keep the windfall earnings that fell to them as a result of increasing oil prices, they would go out and find more oil. As it turned out, to some companies, finding more oil meant using their extra cash to acquire other oil companies.

Factors in Valuing a Merger or Acquisition Prospect

When the seeker and the sought tentatively agree on an acquisition, the usually difficult problem arises of placing a value on the firm to be acquired. In theory, its value depends on the earnings it will bring to the acquiring firm in the coming years. Under any circumstances, it is difficult to estimate future earnings. In a merger, which frequently brings changes in manufacturing, marketing strategy, and management, the problem is greatly compounded. Here are some of the factors taken into account.

Book Value

In this case *book value* means the equity of the company being acquired. This amount, you'll recall from Chapter 3, is the assets' historical cost less their accumulated depreciation and less the firm's liabilities.

Appraised Value

An independent appraiser may be called in to estimate the market value or the replacement cost of the company's major assets. Often, it is some of those assets that led to the acquisition talk in the first place.

Market Value of the Stock

The stock's market value is in itself an appraisal of the firm's value by the investing public. However, as Benjamin Graham, a renowned teacher of investment analysis, was fond of pointing out, the stock market is not a "weighing machine" where precise values are measured. Rather, it is a "voting machine" through which investors express not only their most thoughtful judgments but also their hopes and fears.

Historic and Current Earnings

The firm's earnings are examined for trends that may provide clues to future profits. Such past figures reveal the future about as accurately as an individual's past salaries indicate his or her future earnings. These numbers give you nothing you can bank on, but they may be enough to make a good guess.

Impact of Acquisition on Acquiring Firm's EPS

The company that is doing the acquiring is sensitive to the impact the purchase will have on its current earnings. In many cases, the primary reason for an acquisition is to improve the acquirer's earnings per share. But now and then, a firm will even acquire another that is losing money if it foresees an unusual opportunity arising out of the combination.

How Mergers and Acquisitions Are Accomplished

Mergers and acquisitions are financed in about half a dozen different ways. Most popular is the exchange of common stock, with the acquiring company getting all or enough of the acquiree's stock to control it without losing control of its own. The acquiring company may buy up some of its own stock in order to have it to trade, or it may issue additional common stock.

Fairly often, instead of common stock, the acquirer will issue preferred stock or bonds, usually convertible into common stock, as payment for the acquisition. Occasionally it will pay cash, or part cash and part stock, to the selling investors.

However, transactions involving cash have two negative aspects. First, they create a "taxable event" for the sellers, whereas an exchange of common stock normally does not. Second, the cash paid out represents a loss of funds among the combined companies. Moreover, the loss is often accompanied by increased debt as the buyer borrows the money needed to make the purchase.

A typical approach to negotiations is for the executives of one firm—usually, but not always, the acquiring company—to pay a friendly call on the executives of the other. But when there is opposition to the offer, the buying firm may choose to make a tender offer directly to the shareholders of the other corporation.

A *tender offer* is an offer to buy stock at a given price—usually a few dollars a share more than the current market price—provided a sufficient number of shares (at least enough for control) is made available, or tendered. Such tactics have worked fairly well in the past, but there have been some notable failures, too.

Such a failure occurred in 1982, when the Bendix Corporation sought to acquire Martin Marietta. Management of the latter firm promptly turned on its suitor and began buying Bendix stock in an attempt to acquire the acquirer. The contest ended with Bendix itself being acquired by a third corporation and with Bendix and Martin Marietta each negotiating to resell the shares of the other it had bought in order to pay off the enormous debts it had contracted.

The most sought-after element in a merger or acquisition is synergy—a combination that adds up to more than the sum of the two parts. Synergy means that the merged pair can do more than each could do on its own. It is the grace of all good marriages, as well as good mergers; when it is achieved, value is created seemingly out of thin air.

SIMPLE METHODS FOR
MEASURING INVESTMENT OPPORTUNITIES

As with the analysis of a potential acquisition, the analysis of a new investment focuses on ROI. (By "new investment" we mean any spending of money by a business with the expectation of getting back that money plus some more.) There may be other reasons to make a new invest-ment—such as to meet government regulations, ensure a future source of supply, or console an ego—but most often ROI is the principal reason and, in any event, is always an important one.

Such investments are usually referred to as *capital expenditures,* and there are three or four popular methods of measuring their expected re-turns. Explaining these methods is easier with an example. So let's as-sume we are with a company that has a popular product. We are easily selling all that we manufacture and have $200,000 to expand our produc-tion. Our engineers have proposed that we buy one of two types of equip-ment to manufacture more product, each machine costing $200,000 but with some difference in output. Being imaginative, we'll call them Ma-chine A and Machine B. Here are comparison charts for the two (dollars in thousands):

			Year			
Machine A	0	1	2	3	4	5
Net income from additional sales		$ 20	$ 20	$20	$20	$20
Add back depreciation		40	40	40	40	40
Cash flow		60	60	60	60	60
Investment	$200	160	120	80	40	0

			Year			
Machine B	0	1	2	3	4	5
Net income from additional sales		$ 30	$ 25	$20	$15	
Add back depreciation		50	50	50	50	
Cash flow		80	75	70	65	
Investment	$200	150	100	50	0	

Machine A wears out in five years; hence, we depreciate it $40,000 per year on a straight-line basis. The amount of our investment drops as we recover the cash represented by depreciation. Machine B provides more income in the early years, but lasts only four years. The question is, Which machine is the better investment? Before we get into the analysis, which do you *think* is better? Now, let's see if you're right.

The Payback Method

The *payback method* is deceptively simple. It asks the question, How soon do we get our investment back? Not, How much profit will we make or How long will we make it, but simply, How soon before we get back the $200,000 we spent in year 0 (time present)?

The cash we get back is the profit plus the unspent depreciation charge—or cash flow. For Machine A, cash flow is $60,000 per year. By the end of year 3, this machine will have returned $180,000. About one-third of the way through year 4, we will have recovered our original outlay of $200,000. Machine B returns $155,000 by the end of year 2, and another $70,000 is expected in year 3. So about two-thirds of the way into the year, we should have the full $200,000. Machine A's payback period is 3.3 years; Machine B's is 2.6 years. Thus, the conclusion of the payback analysis is that Machine B is better.

That's all there is to the payback method. Despite its lack of sophistication, payback is a very popular technique for analyzing capital expenditures. Most companies that use more elaborate methods use this one as well.

Payback's main advantage is its simplicity: everyone understands it. But it has a more subtle virtue, too. The forecasting of profits is fraught with error, and the longer the forecast, the greater the chance of misjudgment. Payback, then, tells not only the investment recovery period but also, indirectly, the degree of uncertainty in the equation.

However, payback has a major weakness. It ignores what happens after the investment is recovered. And our real concern is, after all, the profit the investment generated, not simply the recovery of the original amount. Hence, payback is a good tool for rejecting projects, rather than accepting them. And that's why many companies use it as just one of their methods of analysis.

The Average Rate of Return Method

The *average rate of return method,* also called the accountant's rate of return, is similar to ROE. The difference is that this method gives an *average* annual return over the full time period of the investment. The formula for calculating it is:

$$\frac{Average\ annual\ net\ income}{Average\ investment} = average\ rate\ of\ return$$

In the case of Machine A, the net income is $20,000 each year, so the average is $20,000. To calculate average investment, we can use the formula for a simple average:

$$\frac{Beginning\ investment + ending\ investment}{2}$$

In this case,

$$\frac{200,000 + 0}{2} = 100,000$$

Therefore, Machine A's average rate of return is:

$$\frac{20,000}{100,000} = .20, \ or\ 20\%$$

For Machine B, the calculation is a little more complicated. The average profit is the sum of the profits for the four years divided by 4:

$$\frac{30,000 + 25,000 + 20,000 + 15,000}{4} = 22,500$$

The average net investment is again $100,000. Therefore, the average rate of return is:

$$\frac{22,500}{100,000} = .225, \ or\ 22.5\%$$

And so Machine B again rates as the more favorable investment.

The average rate of return method has lost ground in recent times because it does not take into account the time value of money. It counts those profit dollars as if they were all alike, while in fact dollars received earlier in the investment period are more valuable than the same number of dollars received later.

For example, $1,000 coming to us at the end of one year is worth more than $1,000 due at the end of two years, and less than the same amount in our hands right now. The reason has *nothing* to do with inflation. Inflation does affect the value of money, but here we are referring to the *time* value of money, as we explain below.

Present Value Methods

Money we have now is worth more than money coming to us in the future because we can invest it and earn interest on it. By the time the future comes, our money will have grown to a larger sum. To put it another way, money in the future is worth less than the same amount in the present. In business, we say the *present* value of the future money is less than its face amount.

For example, if the current bank interest rate is 10 percent and we deposit $909.09, at the end of one year, with interest added, we will have $1,000. Therefore, the *present value* of $1,000 due one year from now, *discounted* at a 10 percent rate, is $909.09.

The Net Present Value Method

All business investment opportunities involve money going out and coming in over time. The *net present value method (NPV)* discounts these payments; that is, it converts the future inflows and outflows to their present value. Then we total the outflows and inflows—while the outflows are negative, the inflows are positive—to get a net present value of all the transactions.

Here is an NPV analysis of our earlier example. The discount factors in column 2 are the present values of $1 discounted at a rate of 16 percent for the five years after we buy one of the two machines. These values can be obtained from financial textbooks and handbooks, business-type calculators, and many financial computer programs.

We have chosen a 16 percent discount rate as a reasonable return on the company's investment; the rate used is selected by the company doing the analysis. Sometimes referred to as the *hurdle rate* or the *cutoff rate,* it is better known as the *required rate of return*—the minimum ROI acceptable to the firm before it will undertake a project. The amounts in columns 3 and 5 are the cash flows (net income + depreciation), and columns 4 and 6 are the discounted cash flows with the NPVs at the bottom.

When the NPV is a positive dollar amount, as it is with Machine B, it means the investment has earned a return in excess of our discount factor, which in this case, is 16 percent. In other words, the present value of the cash inflows at 16 percent exceeds the present value of the outflows by $5,448. When the NPV is a negative number, as the parentheses indicate it is with Machine A, the investment has earned a return in an amount less than the discount factor, or hurdle rate. The NPV analysis shows

1	2	Machine A		Machine B	
		3	4	5	6
	Present		Discounted		Discounted
Year	Value of $1*	Cash Flow	Cash Flow	Cash Flow	Cash Flow
0	1.000	$(200,000)	$(200,000)	$(200,000)	$(200,000)
1	.862	60,000	51,724	80,000	68,966
2	.743	60,000	44,590	75,000	55,737
3	.641	60,000	38,439	70,000	44,846
4	.552	60,000	33,137	65,000	35,899
5	.476	60,000	28,567	0	0
		NPV	$(3,543)		$ 5,448

*16% Discount Rate

Machine B giving the higher return. Moreover, its return is higher than the hurdle rate we selected.

The NPV requires the use of tables of discount factors and is a little more complicated than the payback and the average rate of return methods. However, it has won strong support among business professionals as being perhaps the "purest" form of ROI we know how to calculate—one that takes into account the time value of money.

The Internal Rate of Return Method

The *internal rate of return method (IRR)* is a variation of the net present value method. Instead of giving us a positive or negative dollar figure calculated on the basis of a company's required rate of return, this method tells us the actual rate of return that was earned; the answer is a percentage.

You saw just above that a positive NPV meant that the ROI exceeded the hurdle rate, while a negative NPV meant that the ROI was short of that goal. If an NPV turns out equal to 0, it means the rate of return is precisely the same as the discount factor. And the rate of return at which the NPV equals 0 is called the IRR.

To determine the IRR, then, we try different discount factors to find one that will give us an NPV of 0. The higher the discount rate, the lower the present value of future cash flows. So if we have a positive NPV at 16 percent, we might reduce it or make it negative with a discount rate of 17 percent or 18 percent. In contrast, we might raise the NPV by using a lower discount rate.

Notice how the NPV is affected when we try different discount factors on our two machines.

Discount Rate	Net Present Values	
	Machine A	Machine B
15%	$ 1,129	$ 9,466
16	(3,543)	5,448
17	(8,039)	1,558
18	(12,370)	(2,209)

Can you estimate the IRR for the two projects? Machine A earns a little over 15 percent. Machine B has an IRR in excess of 17 percent; it's about one-third of the way toward 18 percent. Here are the answers, generated by a computer: Machine A's IRR is 15.2 percent, while Machine B's is 17.3 percent.

You can use present value tables, a calculator, or a computer to find an IRR. However, it's much easier to do with a calculator or computer than to "plug and chug" with the tables.

While the IRR method shares the advantage of an awareness of the time value of money with the NPV method, it has a disadvantage you should be aware of: it assumes that the money earned in the project's first year is reinvested at the same rate throughout the life of the project. If the IRR is 16 percent, that may be a reasonable assumption. At 35 percent, however, it would be questionable.

Chapter 12

Managing Risk and Uncertainty

Much has been made of management judgment in business—mostly by managers themselves. Judgment is that combination of good sense and know-how that is supposed to distinguish the leaders from the led. Although most managers shudder at the association, good business judgment is little more than seasoned intuition.

Intuition—or judgment, if you're more comfortable with that term—is one of our most powerful management tools. Judgment enables us to perceive relationships—as, for example, between price and demand. Judgment allows us to compare alternatives, as between the cost of a machine and the cost of labor. And it equips us to make choices among several courses of action.

Yet just how that process works is still a mystery. We don't know, for instance, how to *develop* judgment except through experience—an expensive tutor who gives the test first and the lesson afterward.

It seems that most of the ordinary decisions in life are made on the basis of crude estimates and guesses. Seldom do we bother to get accurate and extensive information about the alternatives we are dealing with. Even with important decisions such as the schools our children attend and the houses we buy, our knowledge tends to be superficial.

The mental process by which practical decisions are made is very obscure. Frank H. Knight, a recognized authority in the field of logic and decision making, has described the process this way: We are apt "to do a lot of irrelevant mental rambling, and the first thing we know we find that we have made up our minds." No doubt there is some kind of analysis going on in our heads. We draw on past experience for an analogy to the present situation, much as we guess the weight of a package we want to mail—by recalling the known weights of objects we have hefted in the past.

Most of our concrete thinking and decision making is based on analogy, although feelings and logic have their influence, too. The ability to see the similarities of function between things that are otherwise different multiplies the value of our experiences. But our capacity to analogize can also lead us astray now and then, particularly if we are undisciplined about it. Drawing analogies too quickly or impulsively, says Knight, explains "the almost universal prevalence of superstitions. Any coincidence that strikes attention is likely to be elevated into a law of nature."

Perhaps the most useful aspect of intuition or judgment—especially in business—is our ability to predict an outcome when confronted by a novel combination of events. Many animals have the ability to predict on the basis of past experience; Pavlov's dogs salivated when they heard the rattling of dishes. But only human beings are able to put together seemingly unrelated elements to form a picture of future events.

This ability to imagine the future is the key factor in certain of the financial decisions we make in business. All decisions are made under one of three conditions:

- *Certainty*—when we know all the possible results and merely select the one that best suits us.
- *Risk*—when all possible outcomes and the probability of their occurrence is known, but we're not sure what will happen in any particular situation.
- *Uncertainty*—when there are many possible outcomes, but we neither know them all nor know the probabilities of the outcomes we *are* aware of.

Over the years we have gradually developed ways of managing decisions involving risk and uncertainty. Mathematics, the computer, and our fondness for measurement and statistics have enabled us to convert some of the uncertainty to risk, and some of the risk to practical certainty. While free enterprise will never be a science, we are decidedly inching along in that direction.

RISK-ADJUSTED HURDLE RATES

In Chapter 11 we discussed the measurement of cash flows as an aid to deciding between alternate investments; you may remember our example, in which we predicted cash flows four and five years into the future for machines A and B. So as not to obscure the point we were then making, we didn't say much about the uncertainty of those numbers. However, our typical cash flow horizon is about six months away on a good day. Beyond that we usually run into a "fog of ignorance and confusion"—as British economist George Shackle puts it. Had it been possible to forecast cash flows to an extent that might be labeled professional, we'd probably never have seen the SST airplane or the Edsel car, and RCA would certainly have thought twice about the videodisc player.

We've already mentioned that the uncertainty about cash flow increases as time lengthens. That's why quicker and fewer profits are often preferred over long-term gains. But the nature of the investment also has some bearing on the matter.

We can easily see that some investments are riskier than others. Buying the bonds of Solar Power, Inc., involves greater risk than buying the bonds of the U.S. Treasury. Since Congress has the authority to print money, it is hard to imagine a case short of doomsday where you wouldn't at least get paid back by the government. Solar Power, however—like any other corporation—runs the risk of bankruptcy. So if government bonds are yielding 8 percent, Solar Power is going to have to offer something higher—say, between 13 percent and 20 percent—to attract our investment.

Another kind of risk differential is often present in the capital investment decisions in business. The most common such situation involves the high risk of introducing new products. On about the same day early in 1983, Apple Computer announced two new microcomputers. One was the Apple IIe, an "enhanced" version of their old warhorse, the Apple II—of which thousands had already been sold. The changes in the IIe apparently cost the company so little that they didn't feel the necessity of increasing the price over the old model II.

The other new product was Lisa, a brand-new computer, much more powerful and complex than anything Apple had built before. It included innovations such as the "mouse," a hand-held roller ball for moving the cursor and data around on the monitor. According to news reports, Apple had invested an astonishing 200 worker-years of time in developing Lisa, and the $10,000 price tag necessary to recoup the R&D expense put the unit in the Cadillac class among personal computers.

It is obvious that Apple's risk with Lisa was much greater. That's not only because of the enormous cost of developing the new unit. There were also the questions of whether Lisa would work right, whether people would pay $10,000 for an Apple computer, and whether all those executives who have avoided the personal computer because they can't type would be lured to it by the "mouse."

In planning the new products, therefore, the computer company is likely to have required a much higher ROI in its forecast of cash flows for Lisa than for the model IIe. If they calculated their return by the net present value method (discussed in Chapter 11), they might well have used a discount factor of, say, 20 percent for the IIe and 40 percent for the brand-new product.

This risk adjustment of the hurdle rate is a common practice among companies using present value methods. You will recognize that this is where the intuition or judgment comes in: in the selection of the discount rates. In the example above we chose 20 percent and 40 percent as realistic estimates; that was a guess based on general knowledge judgment. The computer company would use the special knowledge they have of their firm, their industry, and their customers, and might come up with slightly different figures. In the last analysis, however, it is only their best guess—based on judgment—that determines the numbers.

MEASURING RISK WITH PROBABILITIES

A few pages back we spoke of a "risk" decision as being one in which all the possible outcomes and the probabilities of their occurrence are known. With such decisions, the possible outcomes can be expressed quantitatively. They are markedly different from decisions involving uncertainty, where neither all the outcomes nor the probabilities are apparent. With known probabilities, we can arrive at a "best" choice using mathematics.

Suppose a friend offers to bet us on the tossing of three coins. Each time all three come up heads, he will pay us $10. But if any one of the coins comes up tails, we must pay him $1. The chance each time of all three coins coming up heads is 1 in 8. (The chance of a single coin doing it is 1 in 2, and the probability of each coin coming up heads is multiplied by the number of coins when you have more than one coin. Thus, with three it is $\frac{1}{2} \times \frac{1}{2} \times \frac{1}{2}$, which equals $\frac{1}{8}$.) Since we are to be paid $10 each time it happens, we can feel fairly certain about coming out ahead if we play for an hour or two. Our decision to play such a game is based not on uncertainty, but rather on the knowledge that the probabilities are in our favor.

If, in a business situation, we have a pretty good idea of the possible outcomes and probabilities, we can calculate an *expected value* for each of the choices. Expected value is a combination of estimated future profits and probability. Each possible outcome of a venture is multiplied by its probability, and the total of the resulting products represents the expected value of the venture.

For example, suppose we were thinking of making an investment and estimated that there was a 50 percent chance of its earning us $1,000, a 30 percent chance of the profit being $2,000, and a 20 percent chance of earning nothing at all. The expected value would be calculated as follows:

Profit	Probability	Expected Value
$2,000	30%	$ 600
1,000	50	500
0	20	0
	Total Expected Value	$1,100

You'll note that the expected value does not correspond to any one of the expected outcomes. Rather, it says that if we had numerous such ventures, we could expect the average profit to be about $1,100. By comparing the expected value of one investment with that of another, we can see which offers the chance for the larger profit.

Mathematical probability is a tool that finds only limited use in business now. However, it seems to have promise for the future, since our ability to record, store, and interpret data is growing by leaps and bounds. The concept is relatively simple, but the results are often quite beyond our intuitive expectations. Consider just one famous example: The probability that at least two people in a group of only 23 have the same birthday is better than 50 percent.

ADVANCED METHODS OF DEALING WITH RISK

One of the advantages of using probability theory in business is that it obliges us to think carefully about the possible outcomes. The more thought we give a proposed project, the less likely we are to encounter some kind of ugly surprise. Building a *decision tree* is an elaborate process for describing with a chart, and in terms of expected values, the various paths down which a decision might lead us.

A decision tree looks like the victim of a violent windstorm: it's laid on its side with the trunk to the left and the branches sprouting to the right. The object is to project the two or more possible outcomes of each decision, and then the additional decisions to which those lead, and so on until we've described all principal scenarios of the event we are considering.

Figure 12-1 is a simple example of a decision tree. Here we have decided to build a restaurant across the street from the site of a proposed shopping center, and are now deciding what kind of restaurant to build. There is now enough traffic to support a small, $.5 million coffee shop, but not enough traffic for a $1 million restaurant and lounge unless the shopping center is built. The calculation of the various expected values helps us to decide which path to follow. The expected value of the restaurant is greater, but the coffee shop shows the better ROI (expected value divided by amount of investment). However, if the probability increases that the shopping center will be built (producing the condition of "Busy"), the change will favor the ROI of the restaurant, with its larger capacity. To each of the outcomes shown could be added other decisions, such as the choice between equity and borrowed money to finance the project. The decision tree branches out as new contingencies are added.

It is the compound growth of decision trees that is their biggest

Figure 12-1.   Decision tree chart.

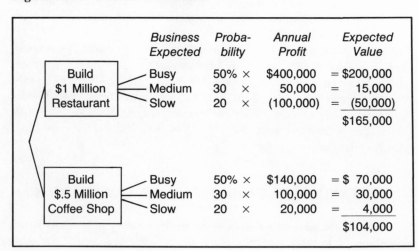

Build $1 Million Restaurant	Business Expected	Proba- bility	Annual Profit	Expected Value
	Busy	50% ×	$400,000	= $200,000
	Medium	30 ×	50,000	= 15,000
	Slow	20 ×	(100,000)	= (50,000)
				$165,000
Build $.5 Million Coffee Shop	Busy	50% ×	$140,000	= $ 70,000
	Medium	30 ×	100,000	= 30,000
	Slow	20 ×	20,000	= 4,000
				$104,000

handicap. There are a seemingly endless number of influences—the state of the economy, the reaction of competitors, and so on—that can affect the final results. And a tree with a mere handful of decision and outcome levels will fill the wall space of a modest-sized room. A decision tree does force you to think carefully about an investment's prospects, but whether that is worth the time and gruntwork needed to prepare it is a verdict the jury is still debating.

Another method for managing the risk of a business investment is simulation, a brainchild of statisticians and computer scientists. With simulation, you forecast a *range* of outcomes rather than a specific dollar amount or probability. For example, you might say the sales from a proposed project will be between $30 million and $35 million. You would then forecast other elements—such as cost of sales, price range, growth rate, and expected life of the project—in the same way, with a range of values for each factor that should cover the most likely results.

Next, a computer would select at random a number from the range you forecast for each of the factors. The sales may be divided into $10,000 increments. On the first run, the computer might select $32,450,000 as the total sales. Similar figures are picked at random from the ranges for the other elements, and from the numbers chosen, a net profit is worked out. The process is repeated with a new set of numbers, and repeated 1,000 times more, or maybe 1 million times. The results when charted will form a bell-shaped curve, with the middle section of the bell indicating the most likely outcomes.

Simulation is an attempt to quantify behavior, and, as with all such attempts, it can hope for only partial success. So long as people cannot predict the behavior of other people (or even, sometimes, themselves), we can't expect a computer to do it. But simulation is kind of fun—almost like a game—and having a result backed up by a million calculations is enough to persuade most people.

Even as statistical methods, such as those that form the basis of decision trees and simulation, are being perfected, we are learning more about the *behavioral* aspects of decision making. A hypothesis first formulated by mathematician and physicist Daniel Bernoulli (1700–1782) states that people base decisions not only on the dollar amounts of the possible gain or loss but also on the relative importance of those dollars. Ask 100 people if they would take the 10-to-1 bet on the tossing of the three coins; even after explaining the sure-thing odds, you will find many who would not. In some cases, the reason will be that while the prospect of winning an average of 20 cents on every throw was not unpleasant, the chance of losing a few dollars in that manner was just awful, and therefore not worth the risk.

PART THREE

Financial Management

Chapter 13

Corporate Planning and Budgeting

Toward the end of the fiscal year, most companies perform an elaborate ritual: the preparation of next year's business plan and budget. This time is typically an occasion for managerial frustration and gnashing of teeth. The aggravations of the moment tend to obscure the value of the process—the value, that is, when it's properly performed, for the business plan and budget are crucial to an organization's success and future profits.

In this chapter we'll focus on these two processes on the corporate level, emphasizing the finance department's role in each. Then in Chapter 14 we'll narrow our focus to departmental budgeting practices and current budgeting techniques.

THE BUSINESS PLAN

Ideally, the budgeting process should begin with a corporate business plan—a statement of where the company plans to go in the future and what specifically it hopes to accomplish in the next year. (The word "statement" is actually somewhat misleading: a business plan may be several hundred pages long.) Some companies short-cut the process by going directly to budget preparation. Budgets alone are better than nothing at all, but the business plan is a useful tool for trying to manage the future rather than just letting it happen to you.

A steadily increasing number of companies now realize this and prepare business plans as well as budgets. Typically, the process begins with an analysis of the company's situation—where it is now in the marketplace, what its strengths and weaknesses are, and even what it perceives its business to be. Now you may think, "Of course, my company knows what its business is." But Theodore Levitt in his classic article, "Marketing Myopia" (*Harvard Business Review,* September–October, 1975), pointed out that one reason so many railroads failed is that their managers saw their business as railroading rather than transportation and, therefore, were unprepared to compete with the growing aviation and trucking industries. Some managers today are equally shortsighted.

The next step in preparing a business plan is to look at the economic environment. The company should include analyses of competitors, technological and social changes that will affect the business, new government regulations, and the outlook for the national and world economies.

After the company has analyzed its situation within its environment, it's ready to develop major goals and objectives, such as increasing sales revenues 25 percent by year-end or increasing return on equity to 18 percent by year-end. Note that these goals are measurable and have specific time frames, not vague rhetoric such as "being more profitable than last year."

One more step remains—a big one: preparing specific, *realistic* strategies for achieving the goals. For example, to increase sales the company might offer its product or service in a new market. The business plan would provide the details—*x* number of salespeople, the advertising plan, the type of organization, and so on. Note, too, that these efforts all cost money, and deciding whether they will add or take away profits is where the realistic judgment comes in.

Planning is difficult, for few future events can be foreseen, let alone controlled. Individual behavior also plays a part. Some people adopt optimism as a policy: aim high and you'll reach high, they believe; and besides, it makes the board of directors happier. Other people feel more comfortable with "realism": it's foolish to kid yourself, they say; what's more, it's easier to surpass modest goals and be a hero.

THE BUDGET

A budget is both an extension or enhancement of the planning process and a powerful control tool. To put it another way, the plan is the words and the budget is the numbers. The budget forces management to convert its plans into specific, measurable terms, and it ensures that the plan's effect on the company's profitability is fully considered.

Budgets can be grouped into two main categories: operating and financial. A company's *operating budgets* are its sales forecast and its production and expense budgets, which are then combined in the budgeted income statement. A company's *financial budgets* are its cash budget, budgeted balance sheet, and budgeted statement of changes in financial position (sometimes called a budgeted statement of sources and uses of funds). Together, these budgets give the finance department a complete picture of the company's anticipated financial position and possible difficulties.

By now you're probably somewhat bewildered by this proliferation of budgets. To reduce the confusion, let's examine each type of budget in more detail and see how they interrelate.

Operating Budgets

The Sales Forecast

Typically, budgeting begins with the compiling of a sales or revenue forecast—expressed both in dollars and in quantities of products or services to be sold. For many companies, this is the hardest part of the whole process. There is no one right way to forecast sales—no magic formula to guarantee success. A method that works for one company may be a disaster for another.

One commonly used method is to survey the sales force and base the forecast on a compilation of their individual estimates. Another method is called "trendfitting"—plotting the historical sales trend to date and projecting it into the future. Many companies combine these two methods to generate the final sales forecast. Other companies use elaborate statistical calculations, which are often based in part on forecasts of economic indicators. For example, one company which manufactures light bulbs obtains statistical data on the average number of light bulbs used in a new house, the forecasted housing starts for the year, and the company's projected market share for bulbs in new houses. This combination of information has proved extremely accurate in forecasting their bulb sales to this market. This technique of using forecasts of economic indicators as a basis for the sales forecast is called "regression analysis."

Another sales forecasting method—called the "Delphi technique"—is based on the principle of consensus. Different groups within the company, such as sales, marketing, operations, and finance, forecast the year's sales and supply reasons for those forecasts. The high and low forecasts are circulated to everyone, along with the reasons for them. Everyone then reforecasts, taking the reasons for the high and low into consideration. If all goes well, a consensus will emerge; if not, the "powers that be" will use the forecasts and the reasons to make a final decision.

We can't leave our discussion of sales forecasting without mentioning one last system: SWAG (Scientific Wild-Ass Guess). Actually, all planning includes some SWAG—and doesn't really involve guessing so much as intuition. In this age of quantitative analysis, most businesspeople are reluctant to admit that they rely on intuition; nevertheless, it remains one of the best tools for sales forecasting.

Production and Expense Budgets

After the sales forecast is prepared, the next step is to determine how much it will cost to provide the goods or services the company expects to sell. Then the expense budgets for the various departments are prepared. Because this is the portion of the budgeting process that you're most likely to be involved in, we'll discuss it in detail in the next chapter.

The Pro Forma Income Statement

From the sales forecast and the production and expense budgets, the company's finance department prepares a *pro forma* (that is, a projected or budgeted) income statement. In fact, the term "pro forma" is frequently used to describe any budgeted financial statement.

The pro forma income statement is similar in style and format to the income statement we examined in Chapter 3. The difference is simply that the amounts on the pro forma income statement are what the company *expects* to earn and spend, as opposed to what it actually earned and spent.

At this point in the budgeting process, a "loop" may develop. If management is not happy with the income forecast on the pro forma, word may go back to the department heads asking them to reduce budgeted expenses by a certain amount or percentage. The sales forecast and strategy may also be reexamined for ways of increasing sales revenues. This "loop" is the reason so many managers dread budgeting, especially when the required revisions call for more belt tightening or unrealistic assumptions.

Financial Budgets

The remainder of the budgeting process takes place primarily within the finance department. A key part of this process is the preparation of the cash budget.

The Cash Budget

As you'll remember from Chapter 5, most businesses use the accrual method of accounting, recognizing revenues when they are earned, not necessarily when the cash is received, and matching expenses to those revenues whenever possible. But businesses, like people, must also be concerned with cash inflows and outflows. It's all very well to record a revenue when the goods are delivered to the customer. However, if you haven't received payment by the time you have to pay your bills, you may have a cash flow problem.

The *cash budget* is a very important tool in avoiding such problems. This budget is based on the time at which the company actually expects to receive payment for its services and the time at which it expects to make disbursements. The cash budget enables the finance department to identify periods when the company expects to pay out more than it will receive and to decide whether it will need to borrow at those times to maintain the desired minimum cash level. The cash budget also allows the company to identify periods when extra cash will be available for short-term investments.

Table 13-1 shows part of a typical cash budget. Note that the budget is prepared in monthly increments. Since this is an estimate, it's not uncommon for a company to work out contingency cash budgets for a number of possible levels of revenue.

The remainder of the budgeting process involves the preparation of *pro forma* versions of the two other key financial statements: the balance sheet and the statement of changes in financial position.

Table 13-1. The Caveat Emporium Department Store Cash Budget.

	January	February	March
Receipts			
Cash sales	$ 75,000	$ 70,000	$ 90,000
Accounts receivable collections	170,000	165,000	150,000
Investment revenues	4,500	4,200	4,400
Total	249,500	239,200	244,400
Disbursements			
Accounts payable payments	178,000	190,000	165,000
Payroll	18,000	18,000	20,000
Rent	4,000	4,000	4,000
Equipment lease payments	1,500	1,500	1,500
Selling, G&A expense	7,000	7,000	10,000
Interest payments	150	—	—
Federal income tax	—	—	35,000
Local tax	—	3,500	—
Dividends	—	15,000	—
Bank loan repayment	10,000	—	—
Total	218,650	239,000	235,500
Cash over (under)	30,850	200	8,900
Beginning balance	93,000	123,850	124,050
Bank loans	—	—	—
Ending balance	$123,850	$124,050	$132,950

The Pro Forma Balance Sheet

Before the pro forma balance sheet for next year can be prepared, the finance department must prepare an estimated balance sheet for the end of the current year. This task is normally not difficult, as the company is already near the end of that year. Then, using the data from the pro forma income statement and the cash budget, the company is able to project the next year-end balance sheet.

The Pro Forma Statement of Changes

Our last pro forma statement is the statement of changes in financial position—the examination of the sources and uses of funds. As you'll remember from Chapter 3, all the numbers on this statement are derived from either the balance sheet or the income statement. Hence, its compilation is relatively routine. However, the statement is significant because it allows the company to analyze its expected sources and uses of funds, as well as to determine the anticipated increase or decrease in its working capital.

The Financing Plan

The cash budget may reveal a need for extensive borrowing, especially if the company plans a major undertaking. Consequently, the budgeting process also includes a financing plan which includes the company's long- and short-term needs for funds for the year, the proposed methods of obtaining these funds, and their cost. In Chapters 18, 19, and 20 we'll discuss in detail the various financing options that are available.

Analyzing the Pro Formas

It is not enough simply to prepare the pro formas and to determine how much, if any, money the company expects to make in the next year. The finance department must also analyze these statements, using the same financial analysis techniques (discussed in Chapter 8) as for actual financial statements. A major part of this analysis is the computation of key financial ratios. For example, the finance department is sure to compute the two key liquidity ratios (current and quick), in order to determine the company's anticipated position in this area. And if any of the ratios indicate potential problems, the financing plan and budget may have to be modified. Forecasting often turns up financial pitfalls—such as too heavy a reliance on borrowing—that might not otherwise be noticed until too late.

Chapter 14

Budgeting Systems and Procedures

In the last chapter we provided an overview of the planning and budgeting process. Here we'll turn our attention to the departmental budget, which in ways large and small affects every person in a given department.

BUDGETING SYSTEMS

Unfortunately, all too many managers try to simplify the budgeting process by adopting the expedient of adding 10 percent (or some other percentage) to this year's costs in order to obtain next year's budget. In an effort to dissuade managers from this type of superficial thinking, many companies have adopted highly structured budgeting systems.

Zero-Base Budgeting

Thanks in large part to former President Jimmy Carter, one of its best-known proponents, *zero-base budgeting (ZBB)* rose to prominence in the mid-1970s. The idea behind ZBB is a simple one. Each department or work unit is required to justify all of its budgeted expenses. Presumably, unnecessary expenses are impossible to justify properly and can thus be easily identified and pruned from the budget. As you might imagine, ZBB did achieve some dramatic savings in government by identifying programs that had outlived their effectiveness.

The other key feature of zero-base budgeting is that managers are required to prepare budgets in increments, which forces them to rank projects and set priorities. Typically, each manager prepares a budget on three levels, or increments. Although these levels are usually numbered *1, 2,* and *3,* more descriptive names would be "survival," "middle ground," and "blue sky." The survival budget is pared to those expenses which are essential to the company's continued existence. Middle ground tends to come close to the current levels of expenditure. Blue sky includes all the manager's dreams. Depending on the firm's financial health, survival or middle-ground expenditures are normally approved, with an occasional blue-sky project being blessed.

In theory, ZBB makes a lot of sense. Justifying and ranking expenses are excellent ideas. When companies *first* utilize ZBB, they usually achieve substantial savings, as the "fat" that has accumulated over many years is removed.

However, problems do arise. First, ZBB tends to generate enormous amounts of paperwork. While this problem can be controlled to some extent, most companies neglect to apply the principles of forms management and paperwork reduction to the program. Thus, completing all the forms is usually very time-consuming and repetitious.

Second, the finance department expands rapidly. After all, people are needed to process the paper and train managers in the new system. As a result, the added expenses incurred in implementing ZBB may offset any future savings.

A third, more subtle problem is that the ZBB system tends to favor the "games player." The manager who masters the complex system and is adept at writing justifications has an advantage over the manager who is less skilled in presenting his or her programs. While this statement is true to some extent with any budgeting system, it is especially so with ZBB because of the system's complexity and the emphasis it places on the justifications.

As a result of these problems, some companies have dropped ZBB; in 1981, the Reagan administration formally abandoned its use—which doesn't mean some future president won't reinstate it. Other organizations have kept ZBB, but in modified form. One popular simplification is to have the manager justify only the 20 percent of the budget containing the lowest priority items. Of course, the company must be alert for the manager who hides the "frills" in the unjustified 80 percent and puts the essentials in the 20 percent.

Bracket Budgeting

Bracket budgeting is the newest star on the financial-management horizon. An integral part of this budgeting system is the computer. First, a budgeting model is developed for each of the company's operations. Then the computer is used to determine how a change in one area or item will affect the rest of the budget. The system also takes into account the probability of a particular number occurring—as, for example, the likelihood of sales of $20 million as opposed to $25 million. The computer makes possible quick budget projections for a variety of situations or "brackets." Likewise, the computer makes it easy to modify a budget to meet changing circumstances.

The computer, of course, can't see into the future. It merely calculates the estimates and ratios that are fed into it. The *quality* of the figures remains tied to the collective wisdom and experience of the people in the department. That's the essence of this—or any other—budgeting system.

Contingency Budgeting

ZBB and bracket budgeting are systems that require corporate support and are implemented throughout an organization. However, the last system we'll discuss here—*contingency budgeting*—can be used by an individual manager, as well as throughout an organization. In effect, it is a mini-ZBB. Like zero-base budgeting, it ranks expenses and involves both justification and incremental levels. However, the process is considerably simpler.

Contingency budgeting is based on four questions:

1. What would cause sales (or revenues) to increase 10 percent? 30 percent?
2. What would I add to the budget under these circumstances? Why?
3. What would cause sales (or revenues) to decrease 10 percent? 30 percent?
4. What would I cut from the budget under these circumstances? Why?

These questions force the manager to relate budget increases and decreases to changes in the business and to rank budget items in categories. The process can be simplified even further for supervisors by supplying them with answers to questions 1 and 3 and asking them to answer 2 and 4.

If contingency budgeting is implemented on a company-wide basis, management may elect to make some budget additions or reductions now without waiting for a corresponding increase or decrease in revenues. If the company does not use this system, it's still a wise precaution for the manager to answer these four questions. It's quite likely that, during the year, he or she will be asked to modify the budget. Such requests are usually made with little warning. If the manager has planned ahead, the revisions will present less of a problem. Without planning, it's only too easy to make a poor decision because of the pressure to meet a deadline.

PREPARING THE BUDGET

The details of the budget preparation process vary from company to company, depending on the system in use. But the basic order of steps remains the same.

Steps in Budget Preparation

First, the manager identifies those activities which must be performed if the company is to achieve the goals set forth in the business plan. Next the manager must estimate the cost of performing these activities. For those actions already being performed, it's simply a case of identifying the increases (or, less likely, the decreases) in the cost of performing the activity next year. For new activities, the estimating process is more time-consuming and more subject to error.

The manager may also be required to rank the department's activities in order of priority. And if the department's activities relate directly to sales volume, the manager may have to prepare budgets for several projected levels of sales.

Even if the company is not on ZBB, we can't stress too strongly the importance of evaluating each expense annually, rather than simply assuming that because it occurred this year, it must also occur next year. This evaluation need not be a formal bureaucratic process, but can simply be a brief review of the activity's purpose and value to the organization.

Expenses have a way of perpetuating themselves, rather like the magazine subscriptions you continue out of habit. But those who think the object of budgeting is to pare every expense to the bone are mistaken. The real object is to find ways to do your job better, faster, and more cheaply than before. In a word, to increase *productivity*. By increasing productivity you create wealth—for the company and, through raises and bonuses, for yourself—literally out of thin air.

The Unwritten Rule of Budgeting

No discussion of budget preparation is complete without a mention of the unwritten rule:

Thou shalt "pad" thy budget because thy company will assume it is padded and will automatically cut it. Thus, if the budget is not initially padded, thou shalt find thyself with insufficient funds to operate.

Obviously, if senior management does *not* follow that commandment, the manager should prepare an "honest" budget, with all excesses pruned. Otherwise, he or she will quickly lose credibility. In fact, systems like ZBB are designed to reduce padding by requiring justification.

Most managers want to be open and cooperative with senior management; they're in the same boat, after all. But occasionally a them-against-us attitude takes hold, and the budget becomes the chessboard on which the two groups try to outmaneuver the other.

THE BUDGET FOLLOW-UP

After the budget is prepared and approved, the company uses it as a tool to measure performance during the year. Typically, a manager receives monthly reports—usually in the form of computer printouts—comparing actual expenses (or revenues) to the amounts budgeted.

Needless to say, the two amounts seldom match exactly. Any discrepancy between the budgeted amount and the actual amount is known as a *variance*. Variances may be either temporary or permanent. A temporary variance is simply a question of timing. The company has incurred the expense sooner or later than was anticipated—as, for example, when a vendor's invoice is received earlier than expected. A permanent variance, on the other hand, involves a change that will not balance itself out later—as, for example, when a vendor, unexpectedly raises prices or when the company overestimates the demand for a product.

Variances are also classified as positive or negative. With a positive variance, the expense incurred is less than the budgeted amount; with a negative variance, the expense is greater. As you might imagine, positive variances are normally desirable—*unless* quality has been sacrificed to achieve the cost savings.

An important part of the budget control process is the requirement that managers explain all significant variances. Some companies require managers to explain only variances that exceed a certain percentage of the budgeted amount—such as 3 percent. Other firms require that *all* negative variances be explained, as well as positive variances that exceed a certain percentage.

In addition to determining and explaining the cause of significant variances, the manager is also responsible for verifying the accuracy of the budget report. In this age of automation, a word of warning is appropriate here: Question any items on the monthly printout that do *not* match your own records (invoice copies, purchase orders, and so on). No, we're not saying that computers make errors, but the people entering data into the computers certainly do. And one of the most common errors is to charge an expense to the wrong account. Such an error is unlikely to be detected by anyone except the manager who receives the charge.

The object of the follow-up is not just to see how good the budget estimates were, but to understand what is happening to the business. Sales are drifting lower—what's the cause? Expenses are creeping up—which ones, and why? Business is a complex of activities that are in sum difficult to grasp. You can work at a place for years and not be able to tell merely by observation whether or not the company is making a profit. Yet profit (or at least the absence of losses) is a condition of any business's existence. The budget variance report gives an early warning of unexpected developments—both opportunities and problems—while the company still has time to react.

Chapter 15

Managing the Company's Money

In these days of high interest rates, cash management has become an important part of the finance department's job. Companies, like people, can ill afford to let their cash sit around, gathering no interest. The finance department's job is to manage this cash—to invest it until it must be used to meet the firm's financial obligations. The department's goals are twofold: first, to maximize the amount of cash available for investment, and second, to obtain a high return on the cash while minimizing the risk of its loss. This chapter explains how these goals are accomplished.

CASH DEFINED

Let's begin by defining *cash*. Obviously, cash is coins and paper currency. But it also includes money in checking accounts—"demand deposits,'' so called because the bank must on demand supply the holder of the account with the currency equivalent of the amount on deposit. And, as we discussed in Chapter 3, the company's cash holdings are listed as ''cash'' on the balance sheet.

SHORT-TERM INVESTMENTS

Because cash in a bank account earns minimal interest, most companies place the majority of their cash on hand in various *short-term investments* (also called marketable securities and temporary investments). These are highly liquid investments—that is, they are easy to convert to cash—and have a minimal risk of loss. However, the general rule is: The higher the risk, the greater the return.

A company seeking short-term investments for its cash has a wide range to choose from. Let's look at a few of the more popular investment choices.

U.S. Government Securities

Treasury bills (T-bills), notes, and bonds are issued for sale by the U.S. government to finance its operations. T-bills mature in one year or less, while the original maturity is one to ten years on U.S. Treasury notes and ten years or more on Treasury bonds. These government securities are very popular because of the extremely low risk factor (the U.S. government guarantees payment of interest and repayment of the principal) and their high liquidity (they can easily be sold for cash). However, as you might suspect, they provide a relatively low return compared to other investment options.

Federal Agency Issues

A number of federal agencies also issue securities to finance their operations. These securities are usually guaranteed by their issuing agencies rather than by the government itself. Consequently, the interest rate is higher than that of comparable U.S. Treasury securities. These securities are also highly marketable. Among the agencies making such issues are the Federal National Mortgage Association (''Fannie Mae,'' for short), the Federal Home Loan Bank, the Federal Farm Credit Bank, and the Government National Mortgage Association (''Ginnie Mae'').

Commercial Paper

Many large companies issue unsecured promissory notes as a means of meeting their short-term needs for cash. Because such *commercial paper* is unsecured (that is, the borrower puts up no collateral), the interest rates are normally higher than for government securities. Finance companies, such as Ford Motor Credit Corporation and General Motors Acceptance Corporation (GMAC), are major issuers of commercial paper.

Bankers' Acceptances

Some companies buy goods with a *banker's acceptance,* which is a draft—like a postdated check—due in three to six months. The draft is "accepted" or guaranteed by their bank, and the holder may either keep it until it's due or sell it in the money market. A banker's acceptance makes a good temporary investment.

Repurchase Agreements ("Repos")

A *repurchase agreement,* or "repo," enables a company to buy a security from a dealer for a specific period—usually a few days. At the end of that time, the dealer will repurchase the security for a specified amount. Thus the investor can obtain a good return for exactly the amount of time the cash is available for investment.

Certificates of Deposit (CDs)

A *certificate of deposit (CD)* is a deposit of funds at a bank for a specified period and at a specified interest rate. A CD is guaranteed by the bank and matures after an allotted time interval that may range from 30 days to a year. Interest rates are usually approximately comparable to those for bankers' acceptances and commercial paper.

Money Market Funds

Many of the above investment options require minimum investments of $100,000 or more. Smaller businesses may not have such large cash excesses to invest. *Money market funds* are an alternative for these companies, as well as for larger firms and for private investors. The various investors buy shares in the fund, and the fund's management then pools their money to buy short-term securities, such as those we've just discussed. The fund's management receives a "management fee" for its efforts, and the investors can either receive cash dividends or reinvest their return in more shares. Since checks can be written on money market funds, they are highly liquid. However, the funds are not government insured or guaranteed.

Most companies use a mix of the short-term investment options we've discussed, rather than just one. These investments will be chosen with the following goals in mind:

- Securing a high interest rate with a minimum of risk.
- Being able to convert the security to cash at the appropriate time.

CASH COLLECTION TECHNIQUES

In addition to selecting the best possible investment opportunities for the company's cash, the finance department must also ensure that the cash is available for the longest period possible. This second goal is accomplished by collecting funds as quickly as possible and by making payments when due, not ahead of time.

Lockboxes and Preauthorized Checks

Lockboxes are one very popular system for speeding the collection process. The customer mails his or her payment to a special post office box. The company's bank picks up the mail and promptly deposits the checks in the company's account. This process saves the time that the company would spend processing the checks and sending them to the bank for deposit. By renting lockboxes in strategic locations throughout the sales area, the company can also reduce the amount of time the check is in the mail. Banks usually charge on a per-item basis for lockbox service. To decide if a lockbox system is profitable, the company must compare the charges incurred with the additional income generated by having the cash available for investment sooner.

Preauthorized checks (PACs) also speed the collection process. Here the customer authorizes the bank to create a PAC monthly and deposit it to the company's account on an agreed-upon date. Such systems are usually used for fixed-amount payments such as mortgage installments. The customer is saved the trouble of writing a check, and the company receives prompt payment. The electronic version of the PAC is the preauthorized debit, the difference being that no paper check is created and the appropriate accounts are simply debited and credited.

Funds Movement

Not only does the company wish to collect the money from its customers as quickly as possible, but it also wants to move the funds quickly to a bank where it has a major account—a so-called bank of concentration. Wire transfer services and depository transfer checks are the most common methods for handling such funds movement.

Wire transfer services permit transfer of funds on the same day from one bank to another. Thus the funds collected by an outlying bank through a lockbox can be transferred to the company's bank of concentration. Depository transfer checks accomplish the same purpose at less cost, but they are slower. A depository check payable to the concentration bank is drawn on the local bank and processed through the normal banking channels.

CASH DISBURSEMENT TECHNIQUES

Another aspect of cash management is keeping cash as long as is legitimately possible before paying it out (disbursing it). To aid in this process, many companies have sophisticated computerized accounts payable systems. Such systems ensure that bills are not paid until they fall due. For example, if the supplier's terms are "net 30" (that is, the full amount is due in 30 days), the company will not send the check in payment until that time.

If, however, the supplier offers a discount for early payment, the decision on when to pay becomes a little more complex. The discount rate needs to be converted to an annual percentage rate. Then the company can compare this rate to the rate currently available on marketable securities and select the higher of the two.

Here's an example. Suppose the terms are 2/10, net 30. This means that the company can either take a 2 percent discount if it pays within 10 days or pay the full amount in 30 days. In other words, the company must choose between taking the 2 percent discount and investing the money for 20 extra days (30 − 10). The following equation converts the 2 percent to an annual rate for comparison purposes. (Note that in figuring interest rates, 360 is conventionally used as the number of days in a year.)

$$\frac{2}{30-10} = \frac{x \ (annual \ interest \ rate)}{360 \ (days)}$$

$$\frac{2(360)}{20} = x$$

$$36\% \ \ = x$$

Since, even at today's interest rates, the company would be unlikely to get a 36 percent return on money it invested, it should take the discount. If the terms were 1/10, net 30, the annual rate would be 18 percent. The choice would be less obvious then, but the company would probably still opt for the discount.

As you've just seen, computerized accounts payable systems are one technique for controlling disbursements. Zero balance accounts are another. These are special disbursement accounts that have no balance of funds. When a check written on such an account is presented to the bank for payment, the bank transfers funds into the empty account to cover the check. This system allows the company to keep its funds under centralized control, while having a decentralized disbursement system. And, of course, funds that would otherwise be held in disbursement accounts are made available for investment until they must actually be paid out.

One other technique used by companies to hold on to their cash as long as possible is remote disbursement. A company writes a check on a bank that is not located near the supplier—using, say, a bank in Utah to pay suppliers in New York. This lengthens the time it takes for the check to clear, allowing the company to keep control of the funds for investment purposes for a longer period. While remote disbursement is not illegal, it does have some negative ethical implications because of the unfair burden it places on suppliers waiting to collect.

Other techniques in use by some businesses are even less commendable. For example, some companies take discounts even though they are making payment after the discount period. And other companies delay payment past the terms agreed upon. For example, they might pay a "net 30" bill in 45 or 60 days.

Such practices, of course, often hurt the credit rating of the company that engages in them. They also force suppliers to take counter-measures, such as requiring payment in advance or increasing prices to compensate for delays before payment is received.

Until recently, one of the more widely publicized offenders was the federal government, which often did not pay on time. However, a new law that requires government agencies to pay interest on bills not paid in 45 days should do much to reduce this problem.

In this chapter we've discussed how the company can receive the best return on its available cash. In the next chapter we'll look at the source of that cash—the company's accounts receivable—and the related area of credit management.

Chapter 16

Accounts Receivable and Credit Management

Accounts receivable are the money a firm is owed by its customers. And unless the firm is strictly a cash business—your local hot dog stand, for example—it extends credit to its customers and, hence, has receivables. In fact, in today's society credit has become a way of life for practically everyone. Consequently, the company's finance department must devote considerable effort to developing the most profitable credit policy and to ensuring that the receivables are paid (that is, collected and converted to cash) in a timely manner. Otherwise, the firm may experience a cash shortage.

THE COSTS OF OFFERING CREDIT

Although we tend to think of credit as "free" if no interest charges are added on, that's not really accurate. A firm incurs a number of costs when it decides to grant credit to its customers. Those costs are passed on to the customers in the form of higher prices. In fact, some businesses, such as gas stations, now reverse that concept by giving a discount to customers who pay with cash instead of credit cards.

One cost of offering credit is, of course, maintaining a credit department. This group decides whether or not credit should be given to a customer and, if so, on what terms.

With credit sales, the amount of paperwork (or should we say "computerwork"?) also increases dramatically. Invoices must be mailed out (giving the Postal Service some revenue) and follow-ups conducted when customers do not pay on schedule. Thus, collection expense becomes a sizable factor for credit sales.

Another cost factor is that a portion of the company's current assets is now tied up in receivables instead of cash. The receivables cannot be invested to earn interest or used to pay the company's bills to its suppliers. And if the suppliers require payment before the company collects from its own customers, it may have to incur the added cost of short-term borrowing.

A final cost of credit is the revenues that are never collected—the company's bad debts. A firm's bad-debt expense will vary in proportion to how readily it grants credit and how well the credit department is doing its job.

SETTING CREDIT TERMS

While credit does have definite costs, it can be used in a positive manner to increase sales and, consequently, profits for a company. It can also help the firm expand its market share and reach new customers. For these reasons, some experts maintain that the credit department should report to the sales/marketing department as well as to the finance department.

A key consideration in a company's positive use of credit is its credit terms: the length of time before it requires payment and the discount—if any—that it gives to customers for early payment. Today the most common credit terms are "net 30"—full payment is due in 30 days from the billing date.

A firm's choice of credit period is affected by the standard practice in its industry. For example, if all its competitors give terms of net 45, the company had better do the same, unless it offers significantly lower prices as compensation for the shorter payment period.

If the firm wants to increase its sales, it may offer longer credit terms than its competitors. For example, at Christmas time some stores use special credit terms of "no payment until February" as a sales incentive. Of course, extended credit terms do not make up for an inferior or overpriced product. But if all other factors are approximately equal, extended credit will increase sales. However, it will also be more expensive to the company than less liberal credit terms. Hence, the credit department must determine whether the profit from the added sales will exceed the additional cost of the extended credit.

Another way a company may vary its credit terms is by offering a discount for payment within a certain number of days (often ten). Such discounts are less common today than in the past. Whether or not a firm offers one tends to depend on what is common practice in the industry. (See Chapter 15 for a discussion on converting discount factors to annual interest rates.)

A practice that has replaced discounting for many firms is the assessment of a monthly interest charge (often 1½ percent) for late payments. Although a number of firms assess such fees, few customers pay and there is a question as to whether they can legally be imposed without the customer's written consent. You'll notice that credit card issuers always have you sign such an agreement before giving you the card.

CREDIT APPROVALS

A firm has two options when it comes to expanding (or reducing) the amount of credit business it does. The first option was just discussed: making credit terms more (or less) liberal. The other option is to change the firm's credit policy so that it is easier (or harder) for a firm to qualify for credit approval.

When a firm is deciding general policy on the granting of credit, as well as when it is deciding whether or not to grant credit to a particular customer, the firm's goal should be maximizing profits, not minimizing the risk of bad debt. In other words, the more liberal a firm's credit policy is, the more customers it acquires—both good and bad. The credit department should strike a balance between an optimal number of profitable new customers and a minimal number of bad-debt customers.

To implement its policy, the credit department must analyze each applicant's financial position to determine the risk of nonpayment. If the decision is made to grant credit, a limit is usually placed on the amount of credit that will be extended without further evaluation. This limit is known as the customer's *line of credit*.

When making a credit decision, a company has a variety of information sources to draw upon. First on the list is the company's prior experience with the customer, if any. Key considerations are the promptness of past payments and, in the case of businesses, the quality of management.

Another major source of credit information is the customer's financial statements. The credit department uses the financial ratios we discussed in Chapter 8 as an integral part of its evaluation. And, of course, statements that have been audited by a CPA firm have more credibility than those that have not.

In some cases, a privately held company (that is, one whose stock is not publicly traded) may refuse to provide its financial statements to the credit department of the company to which it is applying for credit. This refusal does not necessarily indicate any financial problems. The prospective credit customer may simply prefer to keep information about its finances to itself. However, such a refusal makes the credit department's job much more difficult and can lessen the likelihood that the customer will receive credit.

Another source of data is a credit rating prepared by one of the various companies that specialize in that business. Dun & Bradstreet is probably the best known of these companies. Its credit ratings indicate the estimated net worth of a firm and the quality of its credit. More detailed credit reports are also available. These contain a history of the company applying for credit, information on its officers and the nature of its business, selected financial data, and information on its suppliers' credit experience. The quality of any data collected by a credit rating agency depends on the amount of information available from sources outside the company and the company's willingness to cooperate with the agency.

Yet another source of credit information is a credit check with the customer's bank as to its experience, the customer's average cash balance, loans repaid and outstanding, and so forth. The company or individual applying for credit must grant permission for such a check to be made. The depth of a credit check depends on the amount of credit needed. For a small customer, the cost of a detailed credit check might exceed the profits to be realized from the sale. In such circumstances, the credit department will make its decision from a limited amount of information which can be obtained inexpensively. For a large customer, the analysis will be much more detailed.

CREDIT COLLECTION TECHNIQUES

Establishing even the best credit-approval process is only the beginning; the firm must still collect the money that is due it. The majority of a firm's customers usually pay within or close to the credit terms, but some do not. In the latter case, the firm is likely to begin sending a standard series of credit letters or phone calls. If none of these motivates the customer to pay, then the company will either seek legal recourse or turn the account over to a collection agency. Since these last two options are costly, the firm tries to keep to a minimum the number of accounts that reach that stage.

For some businesses, especially those that are either small themselves or that deal with a large number of small customers, the cost of maintaining a credit department is prohibitive. Yet if the firm does not offer credit, it will lose business to companies that do. The alternative is to offer credit to customers through one or more major credit cards, such as American Express, Visa, MasterCard, Diners Club, or Carte Blanche. The firm performs any credit checks the card company requests, such as calling in for authorization on purchases over a certain amount. The credit card company handles collections, reimburses the firm promptly, and receives a percentage of the sales as compensation for its services.

FINANCING RECEIVABLES

Two options exist for companies that don't want to wait for their cash until their customers pay. The first is to borrow money from a bank or other institution; the accounts receivable are used as collateral. In this case, the company handles its own credit and collection functions. The firm is charged interest on the loan and repays it as the customers settle their accounts. Customers are usually unaware of such loans.

A variation on this technique is for the firm to sell its receivables *with recourse*. In this case, the firm sells its receivables to a third party instead of using them as collateral. The phrase "with recourse" means that the company retains the risk of loss from nonpayment. Since the company retains the risk, it usually handles the credit and collection functions in this case as well.

The second financing option is *factoring*. The company sells its receivables *without recourse* to a third party, called a factor. All bad-debt risk passes to the factor. Customers are usually notified of the transaction, and in that case the factor handles collections; if the customer is not notified, however, the company assumes responsibility for collecting.

ASSESSING THE QUALITY OF
ACCOUNTS RECEIVABLE

Up to now, we've been discussing how a firm manages its receivables. But we also need to consider the quality of those receivables in terms of the likelihood that they will be collected.

If most of a company's receivables are concentrated in a few large customers, the company will want to consider how well those customers are doing. If they are in difficulty, the ill effects would pass through to the companies that depend heavily on their business. Hence, having a diversified group of customers is usually to a firm's advantage.

A company's receivables can be assessed by examining an aging statement. This document states what percentage and amount of a firm's receivables fall into each of these categories:

- current
- 30 days overdue
- 60 days overdue
- 90 or more days overdue

The longer overdue an account is, the less likely it is to be collected. Those in the 90-plus category are especially vulnerable.

The aging statement is an internal document that is not necessarily available to groups outside the company. Another measure of accounts-receivable quality—the collection period ratio—can normally be determined from the firm's financial statements as presented in the annual report.

The *collection period ratio* tells us on an average how many days a firm takes to collect its accounts receivable. Hence, this ratio is better known as *days sales outstanding (DSO)*. It's calculated as follows:

$$\frac{Receivables \times 365 \ (number \ of \ days \ in \ a \ year)}{Annual \ credit \ sales} = days \ sales \ outstanding$$

Thus if a firm has $450,000 in receivables outstanding at year-end and its credit sales for the year were $3,750,000, its DSO would be:

$$\frac{450,000 \times 365}{3,750,000} = 43.8 \ days$$

On average, then, the firm collects its receivables in slightly under 44 days. Is that good or bad? One way we can find out is by comparing the ratio with the average for that particular industry. (See Chapter 8 for more information on industry averages.) If the industry average is 45 days, this company is doing fine. If the average is 30 days, the credit and collection people may be taking life too easy, or the firm may be having collection problems with one or two very large customers.

Now what if the opposite happens and the firm's DSO is much lower than the industry average—18, for example, when the average is 42? Unless the firm offers discounts for early payment, this excessively low ratio indicates that its credit policies are too restrictive. The company is probably losing good potential customers to other businesses with more flexible credit policies.

An alternative to using an industry average is a rule of thumb that says the DSO should be no more than 1.5 times the company's "net" terms. (Some experts use 1⅓ times the net terms.) So if a firm sold on credit terms of 2/10, net 30, its DSO should be 45 days or less:

$$30 \times 1.5 = 45$$

One last comment on this ratio: You'll note that we use annual credit sales as the denominator. If your only source of data is the firm's annual report or financial statements, however, you won't have that figure. Instead you will have to use the net sales figure from the income statement. This number will be satisfactory for many firms, as the great majority of their sales are credit. However, if a company (a department store, for example) does a substantial cash business, you'll need to know the amount of credit sales if the DSO is to be meaningful.

Chapter 17

Stock and Stockholders

The owners of an incorporated business are its stockholders—the individuals and businesses that buy shares in the corporation. Consequently, some of the most important financial decisions for the directors and managers of a corporation concern its stock. In this chapter we'll examine the key characteristics of the various types of stock, the firm's responsibility to make financial reports to the stockholders, and the dividend policy decisions the company must make.

TYPES OF STOCK

There are three main types of stock: common, preferred, and convertible preferred. Voting rights differ for holders of each type of stock.

Common Stock

When a company is incorporated, its charter states how many shares of *common stock* it is *authorized*, or permitted to issue. Most companies authorize more shares than they plan to issue initially. That gives them leeway to issue some or all of the remaining shares at a later date in order to raise more capital for expansion. The firm can also amend its charter to increase the number of authorized shares. However, since this process requires the approval of the present shareholders, it is simpler to authorize more shares than needed when the company is incorporated.

Outstanding shares are those shares which have been issued by a corporation and are owned by the shareholders. If the company later buys back outstanding stock from the shareholders, the shares are no longer outstanding and, as we saw in Chapter 8, are called *treasury stock.*

Now, you're probably wondering why a company would buy its own stock back. There are several possible reasons. The company might want to offer the stock to its employees through an employee stock ownership plan (ESOP). Or it might want to trade its stock for that of another company in order to acquire partial or complete ownership of that firm. Or it might want to increase the price at which its stock is currently being traded on the stock market—its *market price* (also called *market value*). The market price usually rises because investors expect earnings per share to increase if fewer shares are outstanding and thus perceive the stock as being more valuable.

Shares of stock are valued in different ways for different purposes. As we have said, market value is the price of the shares when traded on a stock exchange or over the counter; these shares are all from publicly held corporations. For privately held companies or for companies whose stock is traded infrequently, market price is more difficult or even impossible to determine.

A term you'll frequently hear in regard to a common stock's worth is *book value.* This is simply the amount of common shareholders' equity as stated on the balance sheet divided by the number of shares of common stock outstanding. Common shareholders' equity includes all the money the company received for selling the common stock plus the company's retained earnings.

Book value bears no relationship to market value. A stock may sell for much more or much less than its book value, depending on the investors' expectations for the stock. Theoretically, book value should represent the amount the common shareholders would receive for each share of stock if the company were to be liquidated. Note that we said "theoretically"; that's because the money that makes up the shareholders' equity has been invested in the various assets owned by the company. If those assets were converted to cash, the company would probably receive either more or less money for the assets than they were valued for on the company's books. For example, a piece of land may have increased dramatically in value since purchased, while a computer may have decreased substantially because newer, more efficient models have since become available.

A final type of common-stock valuation is *par value*. As we explained in Chapter 3, par value is an arbitrary value assigned to the stock at the time of incorporation. The par value is usually set quite low (often $1.00 or $1.25 per share). This low value reduces the amount of franchise taxes the company must pay, because these taxes are based on par value.

The par value is also set low because of potential liability to the shareholders. If the company sells the stock below par value and then goes bankrupt, the shareholders would be liable to the creditors for the difference between the price they paid for the stock and the higher par value. However, if the stock is sold above par value—which is more likely to happen when the par value is set low—then the common shareholders' liability is limited to the amount they invested in the company.

Because the common stockholders are the true owners of the company, they assume the greatest risk. If the company were to be liquidated, all of the creditors would have to be paid off and the preferred stockholders reimbursed for their investment before the common stockholders would receive anything.

Common stockholders may receive dividends—financial return on their investments. However, the company is not required to pay such dividends. Later in this chapter, we will further discuss dividends.

Preferred Stock

Preferred stock is so named because its shareholders take precedence over the common shareholders—not only at the time of liquidation, as we've just mentioned, but also in the payment of dividends. Being ahead of the common shareholders in case of liquidation is a dubious distinction, since the likelihood that members of either group will recover their investment is slim.

Owners of preferred stock do have one advantage when it comes to dividend payments. Preferred stock has a fixed dividend rate, which is stated when the stock is first issued. Such dividends are usually cumulative—that is, if the company misses a preferred dividend, it cannot pay the common shareholders a dividend until the preferred dividends are paid to date. A company is not obliged to pay the preferred dividend. If there are no profits, or if the dividend money is needed for an important purpose, the board of directors may decide to skip the payment. Of course, if no dividends are paid on the preferred shares, none can be paid on the common, either.

If the stock is participating preferred, the preferred shareholders receive an additional dividend if the common shareholders receive dividends above a certain amount. A preset formula determines the amount of this extra dividend for the preferred stock. This formula is established when the stock is first issued.

Preferred stock may also have a *call feature,* or *redemption feature,* meaning that the company reserves the option to buy back the preferred stock at a stated price that is always well above the original issue price. This provision allows the company to eliminate the payment of the fixed dividend, if it so desires.

Convertible Preferred Stock

While common and preferred are the most frequently issued types of stock, there is a third category: *convertible preferred stock.* As the name implies, this stock is sold as a preferred stock with a fixed dividend rate. However, the purchaser has the option to convert the stock to a set number of shares of common stock. When the stock is originally issued, this set number of shares is low enough that it is not in the shareholder's interest to convert. For example, the convertible preferred stock may have cost $100 a share and may convert to 3.5 shares of common stock. If the common stock is selling at $20 a share, the investor is hardly likely to convert the convertible preferred stock worth $100 to common stock worth $70.

Both the shareholder and the company hope that the market price of the common stock will rise to such a point that it will become financially advantageous to convert. Hence, convertible preferred stock is an attractive way for a company that anticipates rapid growth to raise money and gradually increase its base of common shareholders.

The dividend on convertible preferred stock is normally lower than that on a comparable preferred stock because of the potential benefits of conversion. Such stock also normally has a call or redemption feature. Thus, when the market price of the common stock rises sufficiently, the company can, by offering to redeem the stock, force the shareholders to convert to common stock.

Voting Rights

Usually only common stockholders have voting rights. That is, it is they who vote to elect the board of directors, who then select the management team that actually runs the company. While this system sounds quite democratic, in practice it is not. The shareholders are often spread out all over the country; they usually own only a very small percentage of the company; and they may not be well informed about the company's operations. For these reasons, existing management can usually retain control of the company by proposing directors whose interests are similar to management's.

Common stockholders have one vote for each share of stock they own. If the stockholder wishes, he or she may attend the annual shareholders' meeting and vote in person. The other, more commonly exercised option is to vote by *proxy*. In this case, the shareholder assigns his or her right to vote to a representative, along with instructions as to how the representative should vote. Management sends such proxy notices to all shareholders prior to the annual meeting.

At times, a proxy fight may occur. In this case, a dissident group of shareholders tries to organize a majority of shareholders and acquire their proxies. If it collects enough proxies, the dissident group can elect directors favorable to its interests and thus gain control of the company or, at least, ensure representation for their viewpoint on the board. Proxy fights are divisive and are much more likely to occur when the company is doing poorly than when it is successful.

Normally all common stockholders have equal voting rights—one vote per share. However, for various reasons common stock may be divided into more than one class—called Class A and Class B, for example. One class may have voting rights, while the other does not. Or one class may have more voting power than another. The class with fewer or no voting rights often has a preferential claim on dividends. The two classes' claims on the company's assets in case of liquidation may also vary. Establishing classes of common stock can, for example, allow family members to retain control of the company by retaining ownership of the stock class with the majority of voting rights. At the same time, the company can raise capital through selling another class of stock that pays greater dividends.

Preferred stock normally does not have voting rights because of the shareholders' prior claim on dividends and on assets in case of liquidation. However, with some preferred stock, the preferred shareholders are allowed to vote if they do not receive dividends for a specified number of periods. Then they can elect a predetermined number of directors—normally a rather small number in comparison to the total number of directors. By the time this situation occurs, the company may be in such financial difficulty that the new directors can accomplish little. Hence, the preferred shareholders' voting rights are usually virtually meaningless.

As you'd expect, holders of convertible preferred stock have no voting rights, unless they convert the stock to common shares.

FINANCIAL REPORTING

As one of its main responsibilities to shareholders, a corporation provides them with regular reports on its financial status. These include three brief quarterly reports and the annual report, which we discussed in Chapter 3. The Securities and Exchange Commission has strict requirements as to the financial and other information the firm must disclose in these reports. This "full disclosure" is designed to protect investors by ensuring that the company does not conceal significant information.

DIVIDEND POLICY

One of the major financial policies that a corporation must establish involves determining what portion of the year's income should be paid to the shareholders as cash dividends and what portion should be kept by the firm as retained earnings.

When making this decision, the company must take a number of factors into consideration. The investors' expectations about dividends are one key factor. The investors may expect the stock to provide them with a relatively steady source of income through dividends, or they may prefer that the company retain most or all earnings. If the company retains its earnings, the investors expect the firm to invest the money wisely in projects that will increase profits and cause the market price of the stock to rise. The investors can then realize a profit by selling the stock or can retain it in hopes of further price increases.

The type of company to some extent determines the investors' expectations. Investors looking for steady dividends tend to select large, well-established firms—such as IBM, Xerox, and ITT—with a history of regular dividend payments. Investors who want increases in market price select rapidly growing firms or those whose stock they feel is undervalued or overlooked by other investors.

In addition to the investors' expectations, the company must consider what uses it can make of the earnings it retains. If the company's current potential uses of retained earnings don't meet its profit standards, then it may be better off paying out more earnings as dividends. If, however, good investment opportunities exist, more earnings might be retained—especially if the cost of long-term debt is high at that time.

Another consideration is that investors tend to prefer stable dividend payouts over wildly fluctuating ones. That's why you often see advertisements mentioning the number of years the corporation has paid consecutive dividends. Many companies also prefer not to raise dividend payouts until they're sure they can maintain that trend in the future. Likewise, some firms continue to pay dividends even though current earnings no longer support dividends. In 1981, in a classic example of this type of situation, General Motors, although sustaining losses and borrowing heavily for new equipment, continued to pay dividends—a decision questioned by many investment analysts.

A firm's dividend policy can also be affected by its liquidity (cash availability) and by its credit standing. Firms with cash shortages and poor credit ratings may need to withhold dividends. In addition, some bond or loan agreements may include limits on the amount of dividends the firm may pay out.

Stock Dividends and Stock Splits

Up to now we've been discussing the payment of cash dividends. Corporations have another dividend option: *stock dividends*. As an example, if a firm declares a 10 percent stock dividend, shareholders receive one extra share of stock for every ten they own. Issuing this additional stock does lower a firm's earnings per share.

Why would a company issue a stock dividend? Well, management may expect the company to grow rapidly and the increased profits to offset the decreased earnings per share. Because of the rapid growth, management may want to conserve cash, yet reward the shareholders; hence the stock dividend.

Stock dividends may also be given to try to obscure a firm's financial decline. The firm may be unable to pay cash dividends and may award stock as an alternative. But such a strategy quickly becomes obvious as investors realize they have more shares of a less valuable stock.

Another, more positive reason for a stock dividend is to lower the market price of the stock and keep it within a popular trading range. For example, a firm may determine that its stock sells best in the $40 to $60 range. When the price reaches $70, the firm may declare a stock dividend, which it calculates will lower the market price to about $45.

A *stock split* is similar to a stock dividend. As an example, a two-for-one split means that the investor now has twice as many shares as before. A stock split is normally made to achieve a substantial reduction in market price per share. The lower price makes the stock more desirable to small investors.

A company may also declare a *reverse split*. As an example, a one-for-three split means that shareholders receive one share in exchange for every three they presently own. A reverse split is normally made to raise the stock's market price by reducing the number of shares outstanding. Such a split may be an indicator of financial difficulties.

PART FOUR

Financing the Business

Chapter 18

Equity Financing

Businesses acquire money for expansion in three ways. The first is retained earnings—the money the business earns through its own operations and does not pay out in dividends to its shareholders. The second method is borrowing—an option we'll discuss in subsequent chapters. The third is equity financing—the subject of this chapter.

As the term implies, equity financing means raising money by increasing the owners' investment in the business—by increasing the business's net worth. The ways to increase equity vary with the type of business—proprietorship, partnership, and corporation.

PROPRIETORSHIPS, PARTNERSHIPS, AND CORPORATIONS: A REVIEW

Before we discuss how these three types of businesses can increase their equity, let's review the differences among them. A proprietorship is an unincorporated business owned by one person. The owner is fully liable for the business debts and can be personally vulnerable if a lawsuit occurs.

A partnership is a contractual agreement between two or more parties. Like a proprietor but unlike a corporation, partners pay income tax on the earnings of the business through their personal tax returns. Like a proprietor, partners have an unlimited liability for the debts of the business, no matter which partner incurred them. The same holds true for lawsuits against the company.

A corporation is a legal entity and is taxed as such. It may have one or many owners—its shareholders. The shareholders are not liable for the organization's debts or losses in lawsuits. If the business goes bankrupt, they lose only their investment.

If a corporation is "privately held" or "nonpublic," the firm's stock is not traded on a stock exchange or over the counter. If the number of shareholders is small—fewer than 25 is a rule of thumb—the corporation is exempt from the regulations of the Securities and Exchange Commission. But because it is privately held, the firm is limited in its equity financing to many of the same sources of capital as partnerships and proprietorships. Let's now turn our attention to these sources.

EQUITY FINANCING FOR PROPRIETORSHIPS, PARTNERSHIPS, AND PRIVATELY HELD CORPORATIONS

The Owners

First of all, the owners can simply invest more money in the business—if they have it to invest. In the case of a proprietorship, this may simply mean transferring money from a personal bank account to the business's account.

For a partnership, there are two options. First, the current partners can dig deep into their own pockets and contribute more money to the business, just as the proprietor can. Second, the current partners can all agree to take on new partners who will each contribute a specified amount of money to the firm. When this is done, the old partnership is, in effect, dissolved and a new one created.

The privately held corporation sells stock to its limited group of investors. The terms of the stock offering will depend to some extent on the conditions specified in the corporate charter. Typically, however, the stock is first offered to the current shareholders, which gives them the opportunity to increase their holdings. Then the stock is offered to selected private investors interested in owning stock in the firm.

This procedure is similar to the taking on of new partners. The differences are that a new corporation is not created and that all shareholders do not have to approve the stock sale.

However, to protect the existing shareholders' interests, the firm's charter will place a limit on the number of shares that can be issued and sold. This limit can be changed only by amending the charter—an action that must be approved by the shareholders.

Venture Capital

The owners of small businesses—be they proprietorships, partnerships, or corporations—may not be able to supply sufficient capital to support their firms' rapid growth. Often the owners have already invested all they can afford to in the business. In this case, there is, of course, the nonequity option of borrowing. We'll discuss this possibility further in Chapter 19.

Another option remains: *venture capital,* funds supplied by corporations, partnerships, and individuals who are willing to take the high risk of investing in small unknown businesses. Venture capitalists invest in hopes of achieving a substantial return on their investment through their partial ownership of the company.

Venture capital is not easily obtained. First of all, the sources are limited. The estimated venture capital funds available in 1982 totaled $1.4 billion—not very much, when you consider how many small businesses were starting up or expanding.

Second, venture capital firms are very selective about the firms they invest in. They're looking for businesses with the potential for rapid growth and great profitability. Consequently, the vast majority of venture capital now goes into high-technology companies, which have this potential. Businesses in other fields may be out of luck.

If a business does interest a venture capital firm, the money may be provided in a variety of ways. One option is a loan—with a share of ownership thrown in. This approach is common for *small business investment companies (SBICs).* SBICs were created in 1958 when the Small Business Administration (SBA) was authorized to license and help finance venture capital companies. An SBIC must put up a minimum of $150,000, and the SBA will double that amount in the form of a subordinated loan. Financing small companies is risky; an SBIC looks to make a killing now and then to cover the many investments that fail. And they sometimes do. Some years ago one such invested a few thousand dollars in the Digital Equipment Corporation and wound up making over $100 million on the investment.

Other options simply call for the venture capital firm to acquire partial ownership of the business through the buying of stock, often preferred stock.

It must be clear by now that a venture capital firm attaches as many strings to its investment as it feels are necessary to protect it. In return, however, venture capital firms do provide more than money. Many of these firms are experienced "hand-holders" who've been through the business development process many times. The advice and expertise they provide can be invaluable to a fledgling business.

EQUITY FINANCING
FOR PUBLICLY HELD CORPORATIONS

When a publicly held corporation wishes to raise additional capital through equity financing, it sells additional stock. However, the process is more complex than for a privately held corporation, as the firm must comply with the requirements of the Securities and Exchange Commission and will probably use an investment banker.

The Role of the Investment Banker

Because most publicly held corporations make new stock offerings infrequently, they are not experts in selling stock. To minimize the risk and simplify the process, a corporation often employs an investment banking firm as a go-between. The investment banker buys the stock from the company and resells it to the public. The difference between the buying price and the selling price is called the "spread" and is the investment banker's profit.

A corporation can offer stock to its investment banker on either a competitive bid or negotiated basis. With the competitive bid system, a number of investment bankers bid for the stock offering. The investment banker or group of bankers with the highest bid wins the offering and buys the stock from the company. If the stock is offered on a negotiated basis, the company selects the investment banker and then works with that firm to determine all aspects of the stock offering, including the price, the timing, and other features that will help to ensure its sale.

The company tends to receive a higher price for the stock with competitive bidding, and the investment banker's spread is lower. For these reasons, railroads and public utilities in some states are required to use competitive bidding. However, with competitive bidding the firm does not receive the investment banker's advice in structuring the stock offering, and that advice can be extremely helpful to a firm that has little experience with stock offerings.

Underwriting

When an investment banking firm buys a stock issue, it underwrites the sale—that is, it assumes the risk. The company receives its money from the investment banker, who then must recover its investment and make a profit by selling the stock to the public. An investment banking firm typically spreads the risk by asking other investment bankers to participate in the offering. The investment banker that is initially involved in the offering usually manages the project and has the largest participation in it.

Sometimes the investment banker sells the stock issue on a "best efforts" basis, instead of underwriting it. This means that the investment banker agrees only to sell as many shares as possible at the established price, and the company retains the risk. This situation may occur with small companies when the investment banker is unwilling to assume the risk of selling the issue.

Securities Regulations

When offering its stock to the public, a company must comply with a number of federal regulations. The government imposed these regulations after the stock market crash of 1929 in an effort to protect investors from misrepresentation and fraud. The Securities Act of 1933 regulates the sale of new securities and requires full disclosure of relevant information to investors. The Securities Exchange Act of 1934 concerns the regulation of securities that are already outstanding; it also created the Securities and Exchange Commission to enforce both acts.

When a corporation offers securities for sale, it must register the offering with the SEC. The registration statement contains details of the offering and the proposed uses of the money raised, the history and financial statements of the company, information about its management and directors including their securities holdings, and various other items of information required by the SEC. The corporation also files a copy of its prospectus with the SEC. This document summarizes the key information of the registration statement and is provided to prospective investors.

The SEC reviews the registration statement and prospectus for the required "full and fair disclosure," which means that the documents must contain all required information and that the information must be accurate and not misleading. If the SEC is satisfied that all of its requirements are met, it approves the registration, and sale of the stock may proceed. If the SEC is not satisfied, it sends the company a "letter of comment." This letter may request additional information or changes in the registration. The company either complies or presents its reasons for not complying. This process usually results in eventual approval, except in cases of fraud or misrepresentation.

SEC approval does not mean that the stock is a "good" or "low-risk" investment. It means only that the information the company provides about the stock is complete, accurate, and not misleading.

In addition to meeting the federal requirements, a stock offering must also have the state's blessing. The state securities commissions regulate the issuance of new securities in their respective states. Their efforts are especially important for stock offerings under $500,000, as these offers are not regulated as closely by the SEC as larger offerings.

Other Reporting Obligations

The SEC also requires the companies it regulates to file annual, quarterly, and special-event reports. As you'll remember, we discussed the annual report in Chapter 3. The quarterly reports provide similar but less detailed information, including condensed financial statements and management's narrative assessment of operations. The special-event report—Form 8K—is filed when a significant event occurs, such as a change in the control of the company, a major legal proceeding, the acquisition or disposition of a significant amount of assets other than in the normal course of business, and any other important event that materially affects the company.

Chapter 19

Bank Financing

Most companies operate on borrowed money, as well as on equity. Banks are probably the most common source of borrowed funds, because companies of all sizes use bank financing; indeed, for small firms banks are often the only recourse. In this chapter we'll take a look at how banks provide that financing, discussing the types of loans that are available and the conditions attached to them.

TYPES OF LOANS

Unsecured Loans Versus Secured

Bank loans can be grouped into two categories: secured and unsecured. With an unsecured loan, the borrowing company does not have to pledge any of its assets as *collateral,* or security on the loan. And, as you might suspect, bankers—a notoriously conservative breed—make unsecured loans only to those companies that they consider quite creditworthy.

With a secured loan, the bank has decided that it needs some additional protection beyond the company's promise to repay the loan. A bank may require collateral because the firm is new and has no track record or because the banker has a few doubts about the firm's ability to repay the loan on schedule. The words "a few" are important because bankers normally do not make loans unless they believe the borrower is virtually certain to have sufficient cash flow to make the repayments on schedule. The collateral is simply an added protection.

Normally, the value of the collateral should exceed the amount of the loan. Then if the borrower cannot repay the loan and the collateral must be sold, the bank should be able to collect the full amount owed it. If the collateral is sold for more than the amount of the loan, the excess funds go to the borrower. If it is sold for less, the bank becomes a general, or unsecured, creditor for the difference due it.

Collateral for a bank loan can take a variety of forms. For example, as we discussed in Chapter 16, a company may borrow on its accounts receivable. Inventory may also be used as collateral for a loan, but not all types of inventory are equally desirable as collateral. Most desirable are inventory items that are relatively standard, don't deteriorate or spoil, and can be sold easily with a minimum of expense.

Loans may be made with equipment or property as collateral, often to finance the purchase of the equipment or property. Such loans are usually for more than one year, while loans on receivables and inventory are generally for less than a year. In setting up the repayment schedule, the banker wants to make sure the market value of the equipment or property always exceeds the balance due on the loan. Here, too, the banker is concerned about the marketability of the collateral. For example, it would be much easier to sell a truck than a highly specialized piece of manufacturing equipment for which there is little demand.

Short-, Intermediate-, and Long-Term Loans

Bank loans differ not only in being secured or unsecured but also in the length of their repayment schedules. A short-term loan is for one year or less; an intermediate- or middle-term loan runs one to five years; a long-term loan is any loan over five years.

Short-term loans are particularly important for firms with seasonal fluctuations in business volume. For example, a gift shop may need a loan in September to allow it to build up its inventory for the Christmas trade. After its customers pay the store in January, it can then pay off the loan. Thus, the assumption behind a short-term loan is that the business's receivables and inventory will convert to cash on schedule and enable it to repay the loan.

Intermediate- and long-term loans are used to finance a company's expansion, new or replacement equipment, renovation, and so forth. The repayment of these loans comes from cash the business generates over an extended period.

Bank loans for a period over one year are custom-tailored to meet the firm's needs and to ensure the protection of the bank's interests. The payment schedule is based, in part, on the borrower's projected cash flow. While equal periodic installment payments are common, other options include paying the loan off in a lump sum and making equal periodic payments with a final, larger "balloon" payment. Among the advantages of this type of loan are its flexibility and the fact that the company does not need to go public with its financial information. And for a business not large enough to arrange other financing, a bank loan may be the only option available.

SBA Loans

SBA loans are a special form of bank loan that is 90 percent guaranteed by the federal government through the Small Business Administration. The loans are for amounts up to $500,000 and are offered only by banks participating in the program. To qualify, the small business must have already been turned down for a loan by at least one bank and normally should have $1.50 in collateral for every $1.00 loaned.

LOAN CONDITIONS

Line of Credit

One major form of short-term unsecured loan is the *line of credit*. As we saw in Chapter 16, a line of credit is the maximum amount the bank will allow a company to owe it at any time. The bank and the firm establish the line of credit for a one-year period and renegotiate it at the end of that time. As discussed in Chapter 13, the firm's cash budget is an integral part of these negotiations because it identifies the firm's financing needs for the next year.

As part of the line of credit agreement, the bank may require that the company clean up its debt for a certain period each year; that is, during the stated period the company should not owe the bank any money. Such a condition fits in with the seasonal nature of short-term financing, as it demonstrates that the company does not need the money continuously but only for a portion of the year.

One very important consideration is that a line of credit is not a legal commitment by the bank to lend the company money. Normally, the bank will honor the agreement and provide the loan. But if the company's creditworthiness slips substantially, the bank may legally choose not to honor the agreement.

Revolving Credit

A revolving credit agreement is a legal commitment from a bank to lend a company money up to the maximum amount agreed upon. The company pays a commitment fee (usually around 0.5 percent a year) on any unused portion of the loan. Like a line of credit, a revolving credit agreement is unsecured. However, it often lasts longer than one year. Another difference is that the borrower has the security of knowing that the money is definitely available if needed.

Loan Agreements

Credit terms are one way the bank has of protecting its interests. The *loan agreement* is another. The loan agreement is a legal document that gives the bank the authority to step in if a company defaults on any part of the agreement. While the bank can demand immediate payment, more often "stepping in" means working with the company to resolve its problems so that it can resume repayment.

A loan agreement is negotiated by the bank and the borrowing company, so the terms vary. However, regardless of the specific terms, the bank will include in any loan agreement both positive and negative covenants as a way of protecting its interests. Positive covenants are requirements that the lender must fulfill, while negative covenants are restrictions on the lender.

One common positive covenant is the requirement that the company maintain a specified amount of working capital (that is, excess of current assets over current liabilities). This requirement is to ensure that the company maintains an adequate cash flow position. Other typical positive covenants require the company to supply the bank with financial statements at specified times and to carry adequate insurance.

A common negative covenant is a limit on the amount of cash dividends the company may pay out in a year. This limit may be either a specific dollar amount or a percentage of net profits. Similarly, the bank may limit the amount of the company's own stock that the company may buy back. In either case, the bank's goal is to ensure that the company does not unduly deplete its cash.

Usually the negative covenants also concern the firm's assets. For example, there may be a limit on the amount of capital expenditures the borrowing company may make in a year. This limit may be a fixed dollar amount or it may be based on a percentage of the annual depreciation. Either way, the idea is to allow adequate replacement and upgrading of the company's assets without excessive expenditures. Likewise, the loan agreement will probably restrict the company from selling off a substantial portion of its assets and from using certain assets as collateral for other loans.

The loan agreement may also limit the amount of leasing the firm may undertake. This is done so that the lease liabilities won't hinder the firm's ability to repay the bank loan. It also ensures that the firm doesn't use leasing as a way to acquire excessive new equipment without defaulting on the loan agreement.

Admittedly, the covenants sound rather formidable. But the bank's goal is not to hamstring the borrowing company, but to protect its own interests by ensuring that the company does not take excessive risks. After all, it is in the bank's best interest for the company to do well and repay the loan on schedule.

Compensating Balance

Another loan requirement that deserves mention is the *compensating balance,* or the amount of money a company must keep on deposit with a bank if it is to be able to borrow money from that bank. This requirement can apply not only to loans but also to lines of credit and revolving credit agreements.

The amount a compensating balance is usually set in some proportion to the amount of the loan or to the amount the bank has committed itself to lend if asked. The compensating balance requirement tends to fluctuate with the availability of credit. If credit is tight, then the required balances are likely to be higher than when credit is readily available.

Floating Interest Rates

A final key aspect of bank financing is the cost of a loan—that is, the interest charged. Interest rates often float—that is, they rise or fall in relationship to some indicator such as the bank's prime interest rate. The prime rate set by the bank supposedly represents the interest rate it charges very creditworthy large companies. We say "supposedly" because, in practice, a good customer's rate may be lower. Thus the interest rate for the loan may be set at prime or at a certain number of percentage points over or under prime. For example, the federal government requires that the interest rates on SBA loans not exceed 2¾ percent over prime. As prime fluctuates, so does the loan rate. Such floating rates protect the bank if the cost of money rises.

Chapter 20

Other
Financing Options

Selling more stock (equity financing) and borrowing from banks are not the only ways a firm can raise additional money. Other options may be long-term—selling bonds and borrowing from insurance companies and commercial finance firms—or short-term—obtaining trade credit, selling commercial paper, and factoring. In this chapter we'll discuss all these options.

BONDS

It's appropriate that we begin our discussion of alternative financing options with bonds, as they are a major source of long-term funds for many large companies. In effect, a *bond* is a loan made by a number of individuals—members of the investing public. While none of the investors could singly provide the money a company needs, collectively they can.

When a company issues bonds, it receives money from the investors in exchange for the bonds. As part of the agreement, the company promises to pay the investors a specified rate of interest on the bond and to repay the principal when the bond falls due. The interest payments are also to be made at specified times.

As an example, on a 12 percent $1,000 bond due in 10 years, the company pays a 12 percent annual interest rate on the $1,000. This interest is paid at specified times, such as every six months. At the end of the ten-year period, the company also pays the investor the $1,000.

Issuing Bonds

Issuing bonds is a process similar to issuing new stock. While the company may issue the bonds itself, it is more likely to use an investment banker that will underwrite the bond offering in much the same way as a stock offering (see Chapter 18). Also, like stock offerings, bond issuances are heavily regulated by the Securities and Exchange Commission, and the company must meet a variety of legal requirements.

However, this is where the parallel between bond and stock offerings ends, for a bond is debt that must be repaid, while the money paid for stock is equity that does not have to be repaid. Stockholders are owners of the company; bondholders are simply creditors. Bond interest is paid from pretax dollars, while stock dividends are paid from aftertax earnings.

Like the bank loans discussed in Chapter 19, bond offerings include a loan agreement, which in this case is called an *indenture*. An indenture contains the terms and conditions of the bond offering, along with any restrictions placed on the company. These restrictions take the form of positive and negative covenants similar to those for a bank loan agreement. Again the concern is to protect the creditors' interests.

Types of Bonds

Bonds come in almost as many different styles and types as automobiles.

Mortgage Bonds

One common category is the *mortgage bond*. As the name implies, specific fixed assets of the company are pledged as collateral for the bond. If the company defaults on its payments to the bondholders, the assets— a building, for example—may be sold to redeem the bonds. As you might suspect, the assets pledged are typically of greater value than the bonds issued on them. Thus, the bondholders have some financial protection if the company defaults on the bonds. If the assets pledged cannot be sold for an amount sufficient to redeem the bonds fully, the bondholders then become general creditors of the company for the remaining amount due them.

Collateral Trust Bonds

A *collateral trust bond* is, in effect, a specialized type of mortgage bond. The assets the company uses as collateral are stocks and bonds of other companies that it owns. From an investor's point of view, the desirability of these bonds depends in large part on the quality of the securities pledged as collateral.

Equipment Trust Certificates

An *equipment trust certificate* is a special type of financing option used primarily by railroads and airlines to make major equipment purchases— namely, railroad cars and airplanes. The bondholders purchase equipment trust certificates, and the proceeds from the sale of these certificates are used to pay for the equipment. The railroad or airline then pays back the price of the certificates plus interest. This series of payments takes place over an extended period, usually 15 years. When the debt is fully paid off, the title to the equipment passes to the airline or railroad.

Zero Coupon Bonds

Zero coupon bonds are one of the newest types of bonds. Unlike other bonds, zero coupons do not provide bondholders with periodic interest payments. Instead, the bonds are bought at a heavily discounted price, such as $250 or $500 for a $1,000 bond. After a specified number of years, the company pays the investor the full amount of the bond—$1,000, in our example.

The term *zero coupon* derives from the fact that many interest-bearing bonds come with "coupons" that the bondholder clips and redeems to collect the interest. But this type of bond has no interest payments, so there are no coupons. Some zero coupon bonds are called *money multiplier notes*. The price paid for the bond is multiplied by a whole number, such as 2, 3, or 4, to arrive at the amount the bondholder receives when the bond falls due.

Zero coupon bonds have one major drawback. The Internal Revenue Service has ruled that although bondholders receive no money until the bond matures, they are to be taxed as if they had received regular interest payments instead of the one lump sum. Hence, the bondholders are in the unpleasant position of paying taxes on money they have not yet received.

Consequently, zero coupon bonds are desirable only in investment situations which are tax-free or tax-deferred. For example, not-for-profit organizations may consider zero coupon bonds a good investment. Many individuals use them for Individual Retirement Accounts (IRAs) and other pension programs because these investments are not taxed until the investor begins to draw out the money at retirement.

Since investors must wait several years to receive any return on their investment, they look closely at the creditworthiness and long-range prospects of companies offering zero coupon bonds. As a result, these bonds are issued primarily by large, well-established companies with solid financial reputations.

Debentures

Debentures are, in effect, unsecured bonds—that is, while the issuing firm pays interest on a debenture and repays it like a bond, no assets are pledged as collateral. Thus, if the firm is liquidated, the debenture holders become general creditors along with the firm's other creditors. Because the purchasers of debentures assume a greater risk, the interest rate tends to be higher than on secured bonds. Also, the companies offering debentures tend to be well-established and creditworthy, because financially unstable firms would find little market for their debentures.

A debenture may be subordinated to some or all of the other debts of the company, which means that the bondholders have a lower priority than the other creditors in the event of bankruptcy, although they would still be paid before the preferred and common stockholders were. As a result, the bondholder is taking a greater risk with this type of debenture.

Both bonds and debentures may be convertible. These investments are similar to convertible preferred stock (see Chapter 18). As with convertible preferred stock, the buyer of convertible bonds or debentures has the option of exchanging them for a specified number of shares of common stock. Both the bondholder and the company are hoping that the price of the common stock will rise until such a conversion is desirable. Thus the company does not have to continue paying interest or repay the principal. And the investor may either end up with a profit by selling the common stock at the market price or keep the stock in hopes of further increases in value or substantial dividends.

Retiring Bonds

When a company repays the principal on a bond, it is said to "retire" it. If the bond or debenture issue has a *sinking fund,* the company regularly sets aside money in specified amounts to provide for the repurchase of the bonds. Such a fund provides protection for the bondholders by helping to ensure that money will be available for the repurchase. In such cases, all of the bonds or debentures will normally mature on the same date.

Serial bonds, in contrast, mature periodically. Some of the bonds may fall due in, say, 5 years, while others mature in 10, 15, or 20 years. This feature keeps the company from having to repay all of the principal at the same time.

Many bonds and debentures—like some preferred stocks, as we saw in Chapter 17—have a *call feature.* This option allows the company to buy back the bond at a specified price before it falls due. This specified price is greater than the mere repayment of the principal and decreases over time as the bond nears its due date.

The call feature gives the company a certain amount of flexibility in managing its finances, although the company pays a premium for that flexibility. If interest rates drop substantially, the company can call in its bonds and refinance at a lower interest rate. As you can see, the call feature works to the company's advantage and to the bondholder's disadvantage. As a result, bonds with a call feature typically pay a higher interest rate than those without it.

PRIVATE PLACEMENTS AND INSURANCE COMPANIES

Companies can borrow long-term money by selling bonds and debentures to the public. Another option is for a company to sell its debt instruments to a single institutional investor or to a small group of such investors—in other words, to make a *private placement* of the debt. By doing so, the firm can reduce or even eliminate the expense of an underwriter by negotiating the price of the offering directly with the buyer.

By placing the debt privately, the company can complete the transactions more quickly, as it does not have to be registered with the Securities and Exchange Commission. The company also does not need to make public the detailed information required by the SEC for public offerings.

Because the initial costs of private placements are lower than those of public offerings, the placements can be made in much smaller amounts. This characteristic can make private placements a viable option for smaller businesses. However, the interest costs of a private placement tend to be higher than for public debt. And the number of lenders interested in private placements is limited, while a much larger market exists for publicly funded debt. Consequently, the firm's circumstances and the amount of money it needs do much to determine whether a public or private debt offering is in the company's best interests.

Insurance companies can serve as yet another source of long-term funding. They now lend money to other companies much as a bank does. Like bank loans, such agreements have positive and negative covenants to protect the lender's interests—the insurance company's goal, of course, being to obtain the best possible return on its investment while keeping its risk to a minimum.

SHORT-TERM FINANCING OPTIONS

So far we've concerned ourselves primarily with long-term financing alternatives. A company also has a variety of short-term choices, in addition to the bank loans we discussed in Chapter 19. For example, commercial finance companies also lend money much as banks do.

Trade Credit

Another short-term financing option—*trade credit*—is frequently used by most businesses. Trade credit refers to the credit terms that a business's suppliers extend. For example, if a firm's suppliers routinely allow it 30 days from the invoice date to make payment (that is, terms of net 30), the firm in effect has a 30-day loan.

Because trade credit is readily available to most businesses, using it becomes part of their standard operating practice. However, although no interest is charged, the cost of the credit extension is frequently passed on to the buyer in the form of higher prices. And, as we discussed in Chapter 15, some suppliers may offer a cash discount for early payment. In such cases, using the full credit terms can be an expensive form of financing.

Commercial Paper

Yet another short-term financing alternative is to raise funds through the sale of commercial paper. As you'll remember from Chapter 15, commercial paper refers to unsecured promissory notes issued by large companies to raise funds for short-term cash needs. In that chapter, we discussed purchasing commercial paper as a short-term investment opportunity.

The other side of the coin is the sale of commercial paper to raise funds. The sale can be made either through a dealer or by the firm itself in the case of companies like GMAC (General Motors Acceptance Corporation) which issue large amounts of commercial paper.

Commercial paper serves as a supplement to bank credit. The interest rates paid on commercial paper are generally lower than those on bank loans. However, a company may not always be able to find an adequate market for its commercial paper. Many firms found themselves in that position in 1970 after Penn Central went bankrupt. Because many investors lost money on Penn Central's paper, they subsequently became leery of commercial paper for a time.

Factoring

One final form of short-term financing, factoring, merits a brief mention here. Factoring refers to the sale of a firm's receivables. We discussed factoring in detail in Chapter 16.

Chapter 21

Leasing

The last financing option we'll discuss—leasing assets instead of buying them—is not a new idea. In fact, leasing goes back to 1400 B.C., when the Phoenicians leased ships to merchants who did not wish to own them. In this country, the leasing of land can be traced back to Colonial days, when Lord Baltimore owned the colony of Maryland and leased the land to his tenants. However, equipment leasing did not become popular until the 1950s. Today leasing has become a major industry, with thousands of leasing companies of all sizes.

WHY LEASE?

The popularity of leasing is quite understandable, if you examine the reasons why companies lease. One reason, of course, is that the firm cannot afford to buy the equipment, land, or whatever and leasing is the only way it can obtain use of the item in question.

Leasing can also provide some significant financial advantages. By leasing, a company can conserve its cash and extend the financing of the asset to a period that is relatively close to the asset's life. Loans, in contrast, are typically much shorter in duration.

In addition, a lease does not require the large down payments that installment-plan purchases frequently do. Likewise, there are no "balloon" payments at the end, as with some loans. Leasing also tends to be a faster, more flexible form of financing than loans.

You'll note that we haven't commented on whether leasing or buying assets is the *cheaper* alternative. That decision depends on a variety of factors. But if the firm cannot take full advantage of the investment tax credit and accelerated depreciation that result from purchasing an asset, it may be better off leasing. The leasing company can take advantage of the tax benefits and pass some of its savings on to the lessee through a lower leasing fee. For not-for-profit organizations or companies that are losing money, this is an especially important consideration.

All the potential advantages of leasing are not financial. By leasing, a company can avoid being stuck with an obsolete piece of equipment or one that no longer meets the firm's needs. For example, many computer leases allow the lessee to upgrade equipment as needed. In these days of high technology, such flexibility is an important consideration. Also, a short-term lease can allow a company a trial period to find out whether the equipment really meets its needs.

TYPES OF LEASES

Leases have become a great deal more complicated than they were in the days of the Phoenicians. This complexity is heightened by the fact that there are two different sets of definitions regarding leases: those of the Internal Revenue Service and those of the Financial Accounting Standards Board. And even with all the rules, leasing cases frequently end up in tax court.

IRS Categories: True Leases and All Others

Let's consider the IRS's definitions first. For tax purposes, all leases are divided into two categories: *true leases* and all others. A company may treat a true lease as an expense for tax purposes and deduct it accordingly. The IRS considers all other "leases" as sales of property, not leases, and requires that the asset be depreciated accordingly instead of allowing the lease payments to be treated as an expense.

While the IRS and tax court rulings as to what constitutes a true lease are quite complex, the main points can be summed up as follows. A true lease lasts less than 30 years. At the end of the lease, the lessee can acquire the asset only by purchasing it at fair market value (that is, not at a discount). When the lease ends, the asset must still have a specified fair market value and economic life left. The lessor must own at least 20 percent of the asset and must receive a reasonable return on his or her investment.

FASB Categories: Capital Leases and Operating Leases

The FASB takes a somewhat different approach to leases, characterizing them as either capital leases or operating leases. A *capital lease* has *at least one* of the following characteristics:

- Ownership of the asset goes to the lessee at the end of the lease.
- At the end of the lease, the lessee has the option of purchasing the asset at a bargain, or discount, price.
- The lease term is 75 percent or more of the estimated economic life of the asset. (Economic life is the period of time during which the asset can be used productively and profitably.)
- The present value of the lease equals or exceeds 90 percent of the leased property's fair market value at the start of the lease. (See Chapter 11 for a discussion of present value.)

If a lease doesn't meet any of these criteria, it's an *operating lease* and, according to the FASB, may be treated as an expense on the company's financial statements, not as an acquisition of property with matching asset and liability entries on the balance sheet. In most but not all cases, an operating lease is the same as the IRS's true lease.

Both the IRS and the FASB really have the same goal: to differentiate between pure leases, in which no commitments are made beyond the length of the lease, and leases that are really agreements to buy the asset or to have its use for virtually its entire life.

Subcategories of Leases

The list of types of leases within our main categories is virtually endless. However, two kinds do deserve mention because the terms are commonly used.

With a *financial lease,* the lessor extends credit to the lessee and transfers to the lessee all responsibilities of ownership, such as maintenance, insurance, and taxes. Such a lease lasts for a period of time close to the item's economic life. At the end of the lease, the lessee usually may either purchase the asset at its fair market value or return it to the lessor.

A *leveraged lease* differs from a financial lease in that several parties are involved, not just the lessor and the lessee. Leveraged leases are normally for assets whose value exceeds $1 million. The lessor puts up a portion of the asset's cost and borrows the remainder from other lenders. Leveraged leases are common for the purchase of major assets, such as airplanes, ships, and production plants.

LEASING AND THE FINANCIAL STATEMENTS

As we mentioned earlier, the type of lease according to the FASB—operating or capital—determines how the lease payments are recorded in the accounting process and consequently affects the firm's financial statements.

Treatment of an Operating Lease

If a lease is an operating lease, the lease payments for the year are treated as an expense. The only financial statement that is affected is the income statement. There the firm's operating expenses increase by the amount of the lease payments for the year.

Treatment of a Capital Lease

However, if a lease is a capital lease, the accounting process is considerably more complex. Both key financial statements—the balance sheet and the income statement—are affected.

Effect on the Income Statement

A capital lease is treated as if the company had purchased an asset and financed that purchase by a loan. This means that two expenses are added to the income statement. One is depreciation on the asset for that year. The other is that portion of the lease payments which is considered interest (remember, the lease is being treated as a loan).

In the early years of a capital lease, the interest expense is a major portion of the lease payments. That's because with a loan the bulk of the interest is paid early in the loan period. (Just look at your car loan or mortgage payments, and you'll see that in the early years you primarily pay interest.) Because of the large interest payments, the expenses recorded in the early years of the lease are likely to exceed the actual lease payments. And, of course, the firm's income decreases accordingly.

Effect on the Balance Sheet

Now let's consider what happens to the balance sheet. The leased item appears both as an asset and as a liability. As you might suspect, these entries may appear under several names. Normally, however, the words "capital lease" will be included in the phrases. Typical names on the asset side are "assets under capital leases" and "capital leased equipment." On the liability side, the entry might be called "obligations under capital leases" or "leases payable."

As the lease is paid, the asset entry is amortized (that is, depreciated), and the liability is reduced. The liability entry is split into two parts: the portion due in the next year, which appears as a current liability, and the portion not due in the next year, which is a long-term liability. So with a capital lease, both the assets and the liabilities of the firm increase on the balance sheet.

EFFECTS OF LEASES
ON THE KEY FINANCIAL RATIOS

An operating lease has a minimal effect on a firm's key financial ratios. (See Chapter 8 for a discussion of these ratios.) The lease payments may increase expenses and lower income. If so, return on equity will decrease. The other key financial ratios are not affected. And, of course, like equipment that is purchased, leased equipment should pay its own way and then some.

A capital lease, however, does have a significant effect on the company's financial ratios. The current, quick, and liquidity ratios decrease because the firm's current liabilities (the denominator in all three ratios) increase through the addition of the lease portion due in the next year. The current assets, which make up the numerators, do not change. Thus, a capital lease weakens the firm's liquidity position.

A capital lease will also have an adverse effect on leverage. The commonly used leverage ratio, debt to equity, will become higher and thus less favorable. That's because the firm's total debt will increase while its equity changes minimally. Therefore, with capital leasing, the firm is more heavily leveraged and may be limited in its efforts to borrow additional funds. Although the FASB rule to capitalize certain leases means that more debt appears on some companies' balance sheets, the overall effect is beneficial. The financial statements and ratios become more realistic indicators of the firm's financial position and are thus of greater value to investors and analysts. After all, leases are often major long-term financial obligations, just as other debts are. Companies must disclose their other long-term obligations; it's only fair that they also disclose these.

THE LEASE-BUY DECISION

One key aspect of leasing remains to be discussed: How do companies actually decide whether to lease or to buy an asset?

Actually, the lease-buy decision is the second step in the process, the first step being the decision to acquire the asset. Once that decision is made, the company identifies the various ways available for acquiring the asset. The decision may be between an operating and a capital lease, or there may be a variety of leasing packages to choose from, as well as a straight purchase. In any case, the company should consider all realistic, available alternatives.

Then, all the cash inflows and outflows for the period of the lease or the expected life of the asset must be estimated. Of course, there will primarily be outflows, as the company is comparing two different expense alternatives—leasing versus buying the equipment. The next step is to calculate the yearly cash flow for each alternative.

When calculating these cash flows, the company must consider the after-tax effect of the expenses or savings. For example, if a company is in the 50 percent tax bracket and incurs a tax-deductible expense of $100, the real after-tax cost is $50. That's because the expense lowers the company's income by $100, and, as a result, the firm pays $50 less in taxes than it would have paid without the expense. So now the company has a $100 expense and a $50 tax saving, and the net effect is an after-tax cost of $50.

After the after-tax costs for each year have been determined, the company must add back depreciation, if any, to obtain its cash flow for the year. Depreciation is added back because, while it was deducted as a pretax expense, it was not a *cash* expense. No one wrote "Mr. Depreciation" a check; thus, the funds are still available. Of course, when the cash flow is being calculated for an operating lease, there is no depreciation and thus nothing to add back.

Finally, the net cash flows for each year of each option are converted to their present values. The reason for the conversion is that the dollars spent in future years cost less than the dollars spent now. The longer an expense can be postponed, the longer that money can be invested at interest. Converting the future expenses to their present values recognizes that fact. For example, $87 today invested at 15 percent will yield $100 a year from now. So an expense of $100 a year from now has a present value of $87, presuming a 15 percent return on the money.

After all the values are converted to the common ground of present value, the company can compare the alternatives to see which will cost the least. However, most companies do not automatically choose the least expensive option. Other factors, like those discussed earlier in this chapter, may affect the firm's decision. For example, much word-processing equipment is leased so that it can easily be upgraded and replaced. The availability of funds may also affect the decision; some firms have no choice but to lease in certain situations.

We've presented a simplified version of the lease-buy decision. In real life, the financial models used for the computations are often quite complex and take a variety of factors, such as risk, into consideration. In addition, each leasing expert has his or her own financial model and supporting set of assumptions and reasons for them. Like financial statement analysis, lease-buy decisions are more an art than a science.

However, regardless of the method used, the goal is the same: to identify the most economical alternative and to take all other relevant factors into consideration before deciding whether to lease an asset or whether to buy it.

Glossary

accelerated cost recovery system (ACRS) A method of accelerated depreciation for tax purposes that became law in 1981. (Chapter 7)

accountant's rate of return See **average rate of return.**

accounts receivable The money a firm's customers owe it; an asset account. (Chapters 3, 8, and 16)

accounting equation An expression showing the essential balance between assets on the one hand and liabilities plus equity on the other. The usual form is Assets = liabilities + equity. (Chapter 3)

Accounting Principles Board (APB) Group that established accounting principles and standards from 1960 to 1973; replaced by Financial Accounting Standards Board (FASB). (Chapter 5)

accounts payable The money a company owes its vendors and suppliers. (Chapters 3 and 8)

accrual accounting A method of accounting that recognizes revenues and expenses when a transaction occurs, which is not necessarily when the money is received or paid out. Compare **cash accounting.** (Chapter 5)

accrued liabilities Expenses for which the benefit has been received, but for which the payment is not yet due. (Chapters 3 and 8)

acid-test ratio See **quick ratio.**

ACRS See **accelerated cost recovery system.**

AICPA See **American Institute of Certified Public Accountants.**

allowance for doubtful accounts An estimate of the amount of receivables that will never be collected, subtracted from receivables on the balance sheet; also called *allowance for bad debts*. (Chapters 3 and 16)

American Institute of Certified Public Accountants (AICPA) The standard-setting professional organization for CPAs. (Chapter 5)

amortization A systematic writeoff process, similar to depreciation, that is applied to intangible assets and capital leases. (Chapters 10 and 21)

APB See **Accounting Principles Board.**

assets What the company owns; its financial, physical, and sometimes intangible properties. (Chapters 2, 3, and 8)

audit   A review of a company's records and financial reports to confirm their accuracy. A CPA audit also seeks to verify that the accounting conforms to generally accepted accounting principles (GAAP) and is conducted according to generally accepted auditing standards (GAAS). (Chapter 6)

authorized shares   The number of shares of stock that a company's incorporation charter permits it to issue. (Chapter 17)

average rate of return method   A way of calculating ROI by dividing average annual net income by average investment. (Chapter 11)

balance   The dollar value of a particular account at a given time. (Chapter 2)

balance sheet   A statement of a firm's financial position; its assets, liabilities, and equity at a certain time. (Chapters 3 and 8)

banker's acceptance   A draft issued by a company and guaranteed by its bank; used as a short-term investment. (Chapter 15)

"Big Eight"   Informal collective term for the eight largest public accounting firms: Arthur Andersen; Arthur Young; Coopers and Lybrand; Deloitte Haskins & Sells; Ernst & Whinney; Peat, Marwick, Mitchell; Price Waterhouse; and Touche Ross. (Chapter 6)

bonds   Instruments of a long-term debt which are sold to investors and which pay a specified rate of interest; the principal is repaid at an agreed-upon time. (Chapter 20)

book value   When applied to an asset: net property value, or an asset's historical cost less its accumulated depreciation; when applied to stock: the amount of common shareholders' equity as stated on the balance sheet divided by the number of shares of common stock outstanding. (Chapters 3 and 17)

bracket budgeting   A budgeting system that uses a computerized financial model to project the effects of different circumstances on the budget as well as to determine the probability of each circumstance occurring. (Chapter 12)

breakeven   The point at which sales (or revenues) equal expenses. (Chapter 9)

call feature (redemption feature)   An option that allows a company to buy back preferred stock at a stated price higher than the original issue price or to buy back bonds at a specified price before they fall due. (Chapters 17 and 20)

capital expenditure   A major purchase (usually of a fixed asset) or an investment. (Chapter 12)

capital lease   A lease that the FASB requires companies to treat as the purchase of an asset and the creation of a matching liability. Compare **operating lease.** (Chapter 21)

cash Coins, paper currency, and demand deposits (the latter refers to money in checking accounts). (Chapter 15)

cash accounting A method of accounting in which a transaction is recorded at the time cash is actually received or paid out. Compare **accrual accounting.** (Chapter 5)

cash budget A budget based on the time at which the company actually expects to receive payment for its services and the time at which it expects to make disbursements. (Chapter 13)

cash flow Most commonly defined as net income plus depreciation; for other definitions, see Chapter 10.

cash ratio See **liquidity ratio.**

CD See **certificate of deposit.**

certificate of deposit (CD) A deposit of funds at a bank for a specified period and at a specified interest rate. (Chapter 15)

certified public accountant (CPA) An accountant who has passed the certification examination given by the AICPA and is licensed by the state in which he or she practices. (Chapter 6)

CFO See **chief financial officer.**

chief financial officer (CFO) The individual who manages the accounting and finance areas of a company and deals with outsiders concerned with the firm's finances. (Chapter 1)

collateral Assets pledged as security on a loan. (Chapter 19)

collateral trust bond A bond secured by stocks and bonds of other companies deposited with a trustee. (Chapter 20)

collection period ratio See **days sales outstanding.**

commercial paper Unsecured promissory notes issued by large companies to meet their short-term needs for cash. (Chapters 15 and 20)

common stock Stock that is true risk capital; dividends may or may not be paid. Common shareholders are the true owners of a corporation and are last in line for compensation if the firm is liquidated. (Chapters 3 and 17)

compensating balance The amount of money a company must keep on deposit with a bank if it is to be able to borrow money from that bank. (Chapter 19)

conservatism The accounting principle that requires that losses be recognized when they appear likely, but gains be recorded only when they are actually realized. (Chapter 5)

controller (also spelled *comptroller*) The individual who serves as chief accounting officer of a company. (Chapter 1)

convertible bonds, notes, debentures, or preferred stock Debt or preferred stock that can be converted to common stock. (Chapters 8, 17, and 20)

corporation An organization formed by a group of shareholders and endowed by state law with the right to act as a legal entity, or person. (Chapters 4, 7, and 18)

cost accountant An employee who records and analyzes costs, especially production costs. (Chapter 1)

cost of goods sold See **cost of sales.**

cost of sales The costs directly connected with making or buying the products a company sells. (Chapters 3 and 8)

CPA See **certified public accountant.**

Cr. The abbreviation of *credit.*

credit (Cr.) An entry on the right-hand column of an account. Credit entries increase liability, equity, and revenue account balances; they decrease asset and expense account balances. (Chapter 2)

current assets Assets that either are cash or will be converted to cash within a year. (Chapters 3 and 8)

current liabilities Debts that will fall due within one year. (Chapters 3 and 8)

current ratio Current assets divided by current liabilities; a measure of a company's liquidity. (Chapter 8)

cutoff rate See **required rate of return.**

days sales outstanding (DSO) The average number of days a firm takes to collect its accounts receivable, calculated as:

$$\frac{Receivables \times 365}{annual\ credit\ sales}$$

Also called *collection period ratio.* (Chapter 16)

debentures Unsecured bonds—that is, bonds for which no assets are pledged as collateral. (Chapter 20)

debit (Dr.) An entry on the left-hand column of an account. Debit entries increase asset and expense account balances; they decrease liability, equity, and revenue account balances. (Chapter 2)

decision tree A chart showing the various results that might come from a decision and the probability that those results will occur. (Chapter 12)

deferred income taxes When applied to an asset account: taxes that the company has paid but that will not show up as an expense on the income statement until later because of the differences in tax and financial statement calculations; when applied to a liability account: taxes that have been deducted on the income statement but that have not actually been paid. (Chapters 3, 7, and 8)

depreciation The gradual "writing down" of a fixed asset; that is, the conversion of it to an expense over a period of years. (Chapter 7)

dividends Money or stock paid to shareholders as a return on their investment in a corporation. (Chapters 3 and 17)

double-entry accounting system A system of accounting in which each transaction is entered twice—as one or more debits and as one or more credits. The sum of the debits must equal the sum of the credits. Double-entry accounting shows the give and the take of a transaction—the accounts that are increased and those that are decreased. (Chapter 2)

Dr. The abbreviation of *debit*.

DSO See **days sales outstanding.**

earnings per share (EPS) A firm's profits for the year minus the preferred shareholders' dividends, divided by the number of shares of common stock outstanding. (Chapters 3 and 8)

EPS See **earnings per share.**

equipment trust certificate A debt offering used to finance the purchase of major pieces of equipment, such as railroad cars and airplanes. (Chapter 20)

equity The amount of the owners' or shareholders' interest in a business; also called *net worth*. (Chapters 2, 3, and 8)

equity/debt ratio Equity (amount invested by shareholders) divided by liabilities (amount contributed by creditors); a measure of a firm's leverage. (Chapter 8)

expected value An amount obtained by multiplying an estimated dollar return by a probability percentage; used in forecasting and capital budgeting. (Chapter 12)

expenses The costs of running a business. (Chapters 2 and 3)

factoring A company's sale of its receivables to a third party, the "factor," without recourse (that is, all bad-debt risk passes to the factor). (Chapter 16)

FASB See **Financial Accounting Standards Board.**

FIFO (first in, first out) A method of inventory valuation that assumes that inventory items are sold in the same order in which they were made or bought, oldest items first. (Chapter 7)

Financial Accounting Standards Board (FASB) The committee currently responsible for establishing generally accepted accounting principles. (Chapter 5)

financial analyst An individual who prepares studies that are the basis for making key financial decisions (lease or buy, merge or acquire, and so on). (Chapter 1)

financial budgets A company's budgeted balance sheet, cash budget, and budgeted statement of changes in financial position. (Chapter 13)

financial lease A lease in which the lessee assumes all responsibilities

of ownership and usually has the option to purchase the asset at the end
of the lease. The lease lasts for most of the asset's economic life.
(Chapter 21)

finished goods   Products that are completed and ready for sale.
(Chapter 3)

fiscal year   The annual period selected by a company for reporting on
its operations. Most firms adopt the calendar year as their fiscal year.
(Chapter 3)

fixed assets   A company's land, properties, plants, equipment, and vehicles. (Chapters 3, 7, and 8)

fixed costs   Expenses that remain constant over the short term, regardless of sales volume. (Chapter 9)

GAAP   See **generally accepted accounting principles.**

GAAS   See **generally accepted auditing standards.**

generally accepted accounting principles (GAAP)   A set of practices
that guide accountants in preparing financial statements. (Chapter 5)

generally accepted auditing standards (GAAS)   Rules that CPAs follow when auditing their clients' records. (Chapter 5)

going concern principle   The assumption (in the absence of any contrary evidence) that a business will remain viable indefinitely.
(Chapter 5)

goodwill   An asset account indicating that the company has paid more
for the assets of another company than their book value. (Chapters 3
and 8)

gross profit   Net sales minus cost of sales. (Chapter 3)

gross profit rate   Gross profit expressed as a percentage of sales:

$$\frac{Gross\ profit}{Sales} = gross\ profit\ rate$$

(Chapter 3)

historical cost   The price actually paid for an asset. (Chapter 5)

hurdle rate   See **required rate of return.**

income statement   A statement of the revenues and expenses of a company and the resulting profit or loss. Also called *profit and loss statement* and *statement of operations*. (Chapters 3 and 8)

indenture   An agreement stating the terms and conditions of a bond offering, along with any restrictions placed on the company. (Chapter 20)

intangible assets   Nonphysical assets such as goodwill, patents, copyrights, and trademarks. (Chapters 3 and 8)

internal auditor   An individual who investigates to ensure that all financial operations are performed efficiently, economically, and ethi-
cally; may perform the same task for all aspects of operations.
(Chapter 1)

internal rate of return (IRR)   The percentage rate of return at which a proposed investment's cash flows are discounted to a net present value of zero. (Chapter 11)

inventory   The items a company has made or purchased in order to sell; a current asset account. (Chapters 3, 7, and 8)

investment bankers   Firms that specialize in handling the sale of securities for other companies, usually by buying the securities and reselling them. (Chapter 18)

investment tax credit (ITC)   A reduction in a business's tax liability, based on the cost of certain equipment that the firm has acquired. (Chapter 7)

IRR   See **internal rate of return.**

ITC   See **investment tax credit.**

joint venture   A partnership or corporation formed to carry out a particular project. (Chapter 4)

journal   A record of all of a business's financial transactions, kept in chronological order. (Chapter 2)

ledger   A record of financial transactions, kept by account. (Chapter 2)

leverage   The relationship between a company's debt and its equity; a firm is said to be highly leveraged when it has a large amount of debt in proportion to equity. (Chapter 8)

leveraged lease   A specialized type of lease primarily for assets whose value exceeds $1 million. The lessor borrows a portion of the asset's cost from other lenders. (Chapter 21)

liabilities   A company's debts and other financial obligations. (Chapters 2 and 3)

LIFO (last in, first out)   A method of inventory valuation that assumes that the items made or purchased last are the ones sold first. (Chapter 7)

limited partnership   A partnership that has at least one general partner with unlimited liability and one or more limited partners whose liabilities are limited to the amount of their investment and who have no voice in the management of the business. (Chapter 4)

line of credit   The maximum amount of money a company or bank will allow a customer to owe it at any time. (Chapters 16 and 19)

liquidity   The time ordinarily required to convert an asset to cash; a company's ability to generate enough cash to pay its bills and expenses on time. (Chapters 3 and 8)

liquidity ratio   Cash divided by current liabilities; a measure of a company's liquidity; also called *cash ratio* and *super-quick ratio.* (Chapter 8)

loan agreement   A legal document that specifies the terms of a loan and protects the lender's interests. (Chapter 19)

lockboxes   Special post office boxes where customers mail payments and the company's bank picks up the payments and deposits them in the company's account. (Chapter 15)

long-term debt   Debts that are due more than one year from the present; that portion of a long-term debt due in the next year is classified as a current liability. (Chapters 3 and 8)

marginal income   The difference between price per unit and variable cost per unit; it covers fixed costs until they are paid, and then contributes to profits. (Chapter 9)

market price   See **market value.**

market value   The price of shares of stock when traded on a stock exchange or over the counter; also called *market price.* (Chapter 17)

marketable securities   Government bonds and other securities that may readily be sold. (Chapters 3, 8, and 15)

matching   The process of recognizing revenues and the expenses incurred to produce them in the same accounting year so as to get a true picture of profit. Thus, manufacturing expenses for goods are deducted when the goods are sold rather than when they are produced. (Chapter 5)

materiality   The principle that financial reporting discloses only significant, or material, information. (Chapter 5)

minority interest   That portion of a subsidiary's equity which the parent company does not own. (Chapter 8)

money market fund   A pool of investors' money that the fund's management invests in various short-term securities. Investments are highly liquid but are not government insured or guaranteed. (Chapter 15)

money multiplier notes   See **zero coupon bonds.**

mortgage bond   A bond for which the issuing company has pledged specific fixed assets as collateral. (Chapter 20)

net income   A company's "bottom line." The word "net" indicates that this figure takes into account *all* revenues and expenses, including income tax expenses. Also called *net profit.* (Chapters 3 and 8)

net present value method (NPV)   A way of calculating ROI by converting future cash inflows and outflows to their present value; calculation requires the determination of a required rate of return and the use of present value tables. (Chapter 11)

net property value   See **book value.**

net worth   See **equity.**

NPV   See **net present value method.**

operating budgets   A company's sales, production, and expense budgets. (Chapter 13)

operating lease   A lease that the FASB allows companies to treat as an expense, not as an acquisition of property, on its financial statements. Compare **capital lease.** (Chapter 21)

operating profit Gross profit minus selling, general, and administrative expenses. (Chapter 3)

outstanding shares Those shares that have been issued by a corporation and are owned by the shareholders. (Chapter 17)

PAC See **preauthorized check.**

par value An arbitrary and usually low value assigned to stock at the time of incorporation. (Chapters 3 and 17)

partnership An unincorporated business owned by two or more people. (Chapters 4 and 18)

payback method A way of measuring ROI by calculating the length of time it takes to recover the original investment. (Chapter 11)

posting The act of transferring transaction data recorded in the journal to the ledger. (Chapter 2)

preauthorized check (PAC) A check that a customer authorizes the bank to create monthly and to deposit to a company's account on an agreed-upon date; usually used for fixed-amount payments such as mortgage installments. (Chapter 15)

preferred stock Stock that has priority over common stock in the event of liquidation and normally pays a fixed dividend; for cumulative preferred stock, the company must pay all missed or currently due dividends before the common shareholders receive any dividends. (Chapters 3 and 17)

prepaid expenses Any expense—rent, interest, insurance, taxes, and so on—that the company has paid in advance; an asset account. (Chapters 3 and 8)

private placement The sale of a company's debt instruments to a single institutional investor or to a small group of investors instead of to the general public. (Chapter 20)

pro forma statement A projected or budgeted financial statement. Sometimes called a *pro forma.* (Chapter 13)

profit and loss statement (P&L) See **income statement.**

profit margin See **return on sales.**

proprietorship An unincorporated business with a single owner; also called *sole proprietorship.* (Chapters 4 and 18)

proxy A shareholder's assignment of his or her right to vote to a representative, including instructions as to how the representative should vote. (Chapter 17)

quick ratio Cash plus accounts receivable divided by current liabilities; a measure of a company's liquidity; also called the *acid-test ratio.* (Chapter 8)

raw materials Any materials or parts purchased from others to be made or put into a company's products; a component of inventory. (Chapter 3)

realization The point in the sales process at which it is assumed that a company has earned its revenues. Usually this point is reached after the goods have been delivered or the services rendered but before payment is received. (Chapter 5)

repo See **repurchase agreement.**

repurchase agreement (repo) An agreement that enables a company to buy a security from a dealer for a specific period of time; at the end of that period, the dealer repurchases the security for a specified price. (Chapter 15)

required rate of return The minimum rate of return on its investment that a company requires before it will undertake a project; also known as the *hurdle rate* or the *cutoff rate*. (Chapter 11)

retained earnings That portion of a firm's profits which is not paid out in dividends, but is kept within the firm to finance its growth. (Chapters 2, 3, 8, and 18)

return on assets (ROA) Pretax profit (or, sometimes, net income) divided by total assets. (Chapter 9)

return on equity (ROE) Net income divided by equity; a measure of a firm's profitability. (Chapters 8 and 9)

return on investment (ROI) A family of ratios that are used to evaluate a business's success and profitability, including return on equity, return on sales, return on assets, and others. (Chapters 8, 9, and 11)

return on sales (ROS) Net income divided by net sales; also called *profit margin*. (Chapter 9)

revenues The money a company receives from or is owed by its customers; often called *net sales*. (Chapters 2, 3, and 8)

reverse split A decrease in the number of shares held by stockholders without a change in the dollar amount of the firm's equity; for example, a one-for-three split means that each investor's number of shares is reduced by two-thirds, but his or her proportional ownership remains the same. Compare **stock split.** (Chapter 17)

revolving credit agreement A legal commitment from a bank to lend a company money up to the maximum amount agreed upon; the company pays a commitment fee on any unused portion of the loan. (Chapter 19)

ROA See **return on assets.**

ROE See **return on equity.**

ROI See **return on investment.**

ROS See **return on sales.**

SBA loans Bank loans of up to $500,000 made to small businesses and

90 percent guaranteed by the federal government through the Small Business Administration. (Chapter 19)

SBIC   See **small business investment companies.**

SEC   See **Securities and Exchange Commission.**

Securities and Exchange Commission (SEC)   A government agency that regulates corporations whose stock is publicly traded. (Chapters 3, 4, 17, and 18)

serial bonds   Bonds that mature periodically instead of all at the same time. (Chapter 20)

shareholders' return on equity   Earnings per share divided by market price per share; the earnings figure used is the expected profits for the future. (Chapter 9)

short-term investments   Cash invested by a company in marketable securities such as T-bills and certificates of deposits; can easily be converted to cash and are treated as cash for the purposes of financial statement analysis; also called *temporary investments* and *marketable securities.* (Chapters 3, 8, and 15)

sinking fund   Money set aside regularly by a company to provide for the repurchase of bonds. (Chapter 20)

small business investment companies (SBICs)   Venture capital companies licensed and partially financed by the Small Business Administration. (Chapter 18)

sole proprietorship   See **proprietorship.**

statement of changes in financial position   A financial statement that shows an increase or decrease in a company's working capital by setting forth the sources and uses of the company's funds. (Chapters 3 and 10)

statement of operations   See **income statement.**

stock dividend   Stock paid to shareholders as a return on their investment in the company. (Chapter 17)

stock split   An increase in shareholders' shares without a change in the dollar amount of the firm's equity; for example, a two-for-one split means that each investor's number of shares is doubled, but his or her proportional ownership remains the same. Compare **reverse split.** (Chapter 17)

straight-line method   A form of depreciation in which the writeoffs are in equal annual amounts; the cost of the asset divided by the number of years determines this amount. (Chapter 7)

subsidiary   A corporation with all or a majority of its stock owned by another corporation, called the *parent.* (Chapter 4)

super-quick ratio   See **liquidity ratio.**

T account   A device for illustrating the debit and credit transactions affecting an account; often used in the teaching of accounting. (Chapter 2)

temporary investments   See **short-term investments.**

10K A report submitted annually to the Securities and Exchange Commission by all companies whose stock is publicly held; contains financial statements and other required information. (Chapter 3)

tender offer An offer by one company to buy the stock of another company at a given price, provided the buying company can acquire a sufficient number of shares to control the other company. (Chapter 11)

trade credit Short-term credit extended by a business's suppliers. (Chapter 20)

treasurer The individual who manages a company's cash, both current funds and future needs. May also be responsible for the firm's insurance needs, pension and stock plans, and credit function. (Chapter 1)

treasury stock A company's own common stock which it has bought back from shareholders. (Chapters 8 and 17)

trial balance A comparison of the total of the debit columns for all accounts and the total of the credit columns for all accounts; the two totals should equal. (Chapter 2)

true lease According to the Internal Revenue Service, a lease that a company may treat as an expense for tax purposes and deduct accordingly. (Chapter 21)

variable costs Expenses that increase or decrease in proportion to sales. (Chapter 9)

variance The difference between a budgeted amount and an actual amount. (Chapter 14)

venture capital Funds supplied by corporations, partnerships, and individuals who are willing to take the high risk of investing in small businesses. (Chapter 18)

weighted average A method of inventory valuation that spreads the cost of the inventory items equally among all units. (Chapter 7)

work-in-process Products that have been begun but are not yet finished; a component of inventory. (Chapter 3)

working capital Current assets minus current liabilities. (Chapters 3 and 10)

ZBB See **zero-base budgeting.**

zero-base budgeting (ZBB) A budgeting system that requires managers to justify all budgeted expenses and to rank them in incremental levels. (Chapter 14)

zero coupon bonds Bonds that do not provide periodic interest payments but instead are sold at a heavily discounted price; also sometimes called *money multiplier notes.* (Chapter 20)

Index